ROB DE JONGH

Food for thought in Exodus

Bite-sized Bible study

WOODLAND PRESS

First published by Woodland Press Ltd 2024

Copyright © 2024 by Rob de Jongh

All rights reserved. No part of this publication may be reproduced, stored or transmitted in any form or by any means, electronic, mechanical, photocopying, recording, scanning, or otherwise without written permission from the publisher. It is illegal to copy this book, post it to a website, or distribute it by any other means without permission.

Scripture quotations from the Authorized (King James) Version. Rights in the Authorized Version in the United Kingdom are vested in the Crown. Reproduced by permission of the Crown's patentee, Cambridge University Press.

Scripture taken from the New King James Version®. Copyright © 1982 by Thomas Nelson. Used by permission. All rights reserved.

Contributions by Peter L. Forbes used by kind permission.

First edition

ISBN: 978-1-913699-06-2

Proofreading by Mary Benson

This book was professionally typeset on Reedsy.
Find out more at reedsy.com

Contents

Introduction	vii
Bite-sized Bible study	ix
The recipe for success	x
Exodus 1	1
Good vs Evil	1
Exodus 2	7
Moses: self-willed and angry	7
Exodus 3	10
The God of Abraham, Isaac and Jacob	10
Exodus 4	14
Moses and Zipporah split up	14
Exodus 5	18
How many signs does it take to believe?	18
Exodus 6	21
No-one listened to Moses	21
Fulfilling the promises to Abraham	22
Exodus 7	24
Respect for those we disagree with	24
Exodus 8	27
Hear him!	27
Exodus 9	31
Unto every one that hath, shall be given	31
Exodus 10	34
Did Egypt survive the plagues?	34
Exodus 11	36

An early warning. Action too late.	36
Exodus 12	39
The armies of the LORD	39
Staying in the house of Jesus	40
Exodus 13	43
Through faith he kept the Passover	43
Exodus 14	46
A name for the LORD	46
Where did Israel cross the red sea?	48
Exodus 15	51
Sweet victory and bitter shame	51
Exodus 16	54
"That I may prove them"	54
Exodus 17	58
"Is the LORD among us, or not?"	58
Exodus 18	62
Sowing the seeds of rebellion	62
Exodus 19	65
Entering into the covenant	65
Exodus 20	68
Draw near, or draw back?	68
Exodus 21	72
O how love I thy law!	72
Exodus 22	74
God protects the fatherless and the widow	74
Exodus 23	77
Balance	77
Driving out the inhabitants of the promised land	79
Exodus 24	81
The hidden man	81
Exodus 25	84

A burden too heavy to carry	84
Exodus 26	87
The structural detail of the Tabernacle	87
Exodus 27	91
Those who had prepared oil	91
Exodus 28	94
Wisdom is more precious than rubies	94
Exodus 29	97
A priest "made like unto his brethren".	97
Exodus 30	100
The perfect incense	100
Exodus 31	106
The master craftsman	106
Exodus 32	109
Joshua, the servant	109
Exodus 33	112
Meeting with God outside the camp	112
Exodus 34	116
Forty days without food	116
Exodus 35	120
Resting from God's work	120
Who is the missing master craftsman?	121
Exodus 36	123
Who gave us our ability to give?	123
Exodus 37	126
Gold that perishes	126
Exodus 38	128
How events are foretold and echoed in scripture	128
Exodus 39	132
The real-life image of God	132
Exodus 40	136

A place no-one could enter	136
Epilogue	140
Other books in the series	142
About the Author	144

Introduction

Have you ever felt like the person standing outside of a window on a cold day, hungry and alone, while inside the house everyone is warm, well fed, loved and full of joy — when it comes to understanding the Bible?

Maybe you have that feeling of embarrassment when you don't appear to grasp a point someone is making, or your friend or family member catches you out by asking you a question you just don't know the answer to.

If that's you, then you can breathe a sigh of relief, because you're in the right place. This book isn't just another Bible study guide, with dry boring academic thoughts that don't help to explain the Bible. It's a bridge between you and one of the most vivid books of the Bible — Exodus.

The story of Exodus isn't just a tall tale of plagues of frogs and the parting of the Red Sea. It shows us how Moses went from a poor slave to becoming a prince in Pharaoh's house, and how he was able to give up all that privilege for the hope of releasing his people Israel from slavery. He had everything you and I have ever wanted, but he was able to give it up in a moment!

How on earth was he able to do that? The New Testament gives us the answer:

> "By faith Moses, when he became of age, refused to be called the son of Pharaoh's daughter, choosing rather to suffer affliction with the

> *people of God than to enjoy the passing pleasures of sin, esteeming the reproach of Christ greater riches than the treasures in Egypt;* **for he looked to the reward.**" *(Hebrews 11:24-26 NKJV)*

This is the way the New Testament teaches about Jesus and about the gospel. It uses these vivid Old Testament examples to draw on, and we are invited to learn about Moses so that we can learn more about Jesus, about faith, and about our own battle with sin.

It's not that we might be entertained, or become knowledgeable, or be better than others. But that we might win against sin ourselves too, in the same way Moses did:

> *"...choosing rather to suffer affliction with the people of God than to enjoy the passing pleasures of sin..."*

And just like you and me, Moses started off far from perfect. As the murderer of an Egyptian, he fled from Egypt, and it took forty years as a shepherd to be humbled and made ready for his great task — the Exodus of God's people, the "Children of Israel".

So I invite you to read on in the book as we discover the wonderful message of Exodus, a book full of the vivid people, places and events that form the bedrock of the New Testament message, and of our own faith.

Bite-sized Bible study

When Jesus taught us to pray "give us today our daily bread", he wasn't talking about food, but the word of God. He said:

> "Man shall not live by bread alone, but by **every word of God.**"

When Jesus met Peter after his resurrection and told Peter to feed the believers, he didn't mean with fish, but with the word of God:

> "So when they had dined, Jesus saith to Simon Peter, Simon, son of Jonas, lovest thou me more than these? He saith unto him, Yea, Lord; thou knowest that I love thee. He saith unto him, **Feed my lambs.**"

Jesus was teaching us that the word of God has to be eaten, chewed over, and thought about. That's why he called us "lambs" and gave the analogy of sheep:

> "I am the good shepherd: the good shepherd giveth his life for the sheep."

We wouldn't starve ourselves all week and then binge eat on a Sunday. That would leave us sick on Sunday and hungry the rest of the time. Likewise, with the Word of God, we need to take some in every day. It doesn't have to be a lot. Just a *bite-sized Bible study*.

The recipe for success

Think of this book as a recipe book, with one meal for every day. Treat it just as you would sitting down for dinner:

1. **Give thanks.** Say a prayer to ask God to help you to read and understand what He has to teach you today.
2. **Eat the main course.** Read the Bible chapter first, taking your time and re-reading anything hard to understand.
3. **Eat the dessert.** Read the corresponding chapter in *Food for Thought in Exodus*.
4. **Chew it over.** Turn up the quoted Bible passages that relate to the chapter, and read them in their context.
5. **Digest.** Go about your day, and when you get a moment, think about these scriptures and any questions or answers they bring up.

Meditating on the word of God every day is the foundation for spiritual growth and health. The Bible is able to make us wise for eternal salvation, and also happy in our lives now.

> *"Blessed (happy) is the man that walketh not in the counsel of the ungodly, nor standeth in the way of sinners, nor sitteth in the seat of the scornful. But his delight is in the law of the LORD; and in his law doth he meditate day and night..."*

And do you know the most wonderful part of all? Just as a tree planted by rivers of water will grow and bear fruit by itself, success is automatic if we do follow this recipe every day.

> *"...and he shall be like a tree planted by the rivers of water, that*

bringeth forth his fruit in his season; his leaf also shall not wither; and whatsoever he doeth shall prosper."

Exodus 1

Good vs Evil

Here at the start of the book of Exodus, there is set up for us a very clear good vs evil situation. Right from the beginning of the creation of mankind, God had given them a commandment:

> So God created man in his own image, in the image of God created he him; male and female created he them. And God blessed them, and God said unto them, **Be fruitful, and multiply, and replenish the earth**, and subdue it: and have dominion over the fish of the sea, and over the fowl of the air, and over every living thing that moveth upon the earth. (Gen 1:27-28)

This is the first recorded commandment from God, even before the commandment not to eat of the tree of the knowledge of good and evil. Thus this explains the primary purpose of the LORD God, namely to fill the earth with mankind.

But mankind has a propensity for evil. When men multiplied, evil multiplied with them, until there was no option but to start again:

> *And it came to pass, when **men began to multiply on the face of the earth**, and daughters were born unto them, that the sons of God saw the daughters of men that they were fair; and they took them wives of all which they chose. ... And GOD saw that the wickedness of man was great in the earth, and that every imagination of the thoughts of his heart was only evil continually. And it repented the LORD that he had made man on the earth, and it grieved him at his heart. And the LORD said, I will destroy man whom I have created from the face of the earth; both man, and beast, and the creeping thing, and the fowls of the air; for it repenteth me that I have made them. (Gen 6:1-2, 5-7)*

When Noah and his sons came out of the ark, God once again reiterated His purpose with this new group of people. In fact, it is the very first thing God says to them:

> *And God spake unto Noah, saying, Go forth of the ark, thou, and thy wife, and thy sons, and thy sons' wives with thee. Bring forth with thee every living thing that is with thee, of all flesh, both of fowl, and of cattle, and of every creeping thing that creepeth upon the earth; that they may breed abundantly in the earth, and **be fruitful, and multiply upon the earth**. (Gen 8:15-17)*

This word is aimed at every animal on the ark, and it is clear that mankind is included, because God reiterates it again to them soon after:

> *And God blessed Noah and his sons, and said unto them, **Be fruitful, and multiply, and replenish the earth**. (Gen 9:1)*

The next wrong step came when people, having multiplied somewhat, refused to spread out over the earth. Instead, they chose to stay together in specific rebellion against God's commandment that they should "replenish the earth":

> And they said, Go to, let us build us a city and a tower, whose top may reach unto heaven; and let us make us a name, **lest we be scattered abroad upon the face of the whole earth.** (Gen 11:4)

The scripture is very specific in giving us each of these events so that we can see the development of this purpose and commandment of God.

So because the people of Babel were going the opposite way to what God intended, God deliberately forced them to spread out over the whole earth:

> Therefore is the name of it called Babel; because the LORD did there confound the language of all the earth: and **from thence did the LORD scatter them abroad upon the face of all the earth.** (Gen 11:9)

As part of that scattering, we are introduced to Abram, who left that place and took a journey to far-off lands. He and his family are the first ones in the whole of scripture to have obeyed that original commandment. Finally, after all this time, someone is willing to be fully obedient to God. So it is no wonder that God immediately promises him many offspring, in other words, to multiply Abraham:

> Now the LORD had said unto Abram, Get thee out of thy country, and from thy kindred, and from thy father's house, unto a land that I will shew thee: And I will make of thee a great nation, and I will bless thee, and make thy name great; and thou shalt be a blessing. (Gen 12:1-2)

This promise comes to Abraham again and again, so that we know that the original purpose of God, to be fruitful, and multiply, and replenish the earth, and subdue it, and have dominion, now rests with Abraham and his offspring:

> *And the angel of the LORD called unto Abraham out of heaven the second time, And said, By myself have I sworn, saith the LORD… That in blessing I will bless thee, and* **in multiplying I will multiply thy seed** *as the stars of the heaven, and as the sand which is upon the sea shore; and thy seed shall possess the gate of his enemies. (Gen 22:15-17)*

The word "multiply" is used each time to make it very simple and clear to us that this is the pattern and theme that God is showing us through the scripture. So when Jacob and his sons came to Egypt, this is what is picked up immediately in Exodus as the book is introduced:

> *And the children of Israel were fruitful, and increased abundantly, and* **multiplied**, *and waxed exceeding mighty; and the land was filled with them. (Exo 1:7)*

Notice how emphatic this phrase is:

- were fruitful
- increased abundantly
- multiplied
- waxed exceeding mighty
- the land was filled with them

It is impossible to miss what we are being told here — God is fulfilling the purpose He had right at the beginning of creation, now with the children of Abraham.

No wonder, then, that the one thing that this chapter focuses on is the birthrate of Jacob's descendants! These people are giving birth at an astonishing rate, so that within a few generations the seventy of them have increased to a number rivalling that of the whole Egyptian nation:

> *Now there arose up a new king over Egypt, which knew not Joseph. And he said unto his people, Behold, the people of the children of Israel are more and mightier than we... (Exo 1:8-9)*

And this is where the good vs evil situation becomes apparent. The king of Egypt begins to fear the very thing that God is seeking to do, namely to *multiply* them:

> *Come on, let us deal wisely with them;* **lest they multiply***, and it come to pass, that, when there falleth out any war, they join also unto our enemies, and fight against us, and so get them up out of the land. Therefore they did set over them taskmasters to afflict them with their burdens. And they built for Pharaoh treasure cities, Pithom and Raamses. (Exo 1:10-11)*

Pharaoh seeks to put a pause on God's purpose and to go against His will. He basically wants to stop Abraham's seed from multiplying. But it doesn't work. God continues His blessing and they give birth all the more:

> *But* **the more they afflicted them, the more they multiplied** *and grew. And they were grieved because of the children of Israel. (Exo 1:12)*

See how anxious Pharaoh and his governors are becoming because of the success of God's purpose with the children of Abraham, Isaac, and Jacob! God is achieving His aim of multiplying them, but now Pharaoh stands in God's way. Not only does he seek to stop them from multiplying, he has also enslaved them so that they cannot go out and replenish the earth. He is going precisely the opposite way to God's will:

> *And the king of Egypt spake to the Hebrew midwives, of which the name of the one was Shiphrah, and the name of the other Puah: and he said, when ye do the office of a midwife to the Hebrew women, and see them upon the stools; if it be a son, then ye shall kill him: but if it be a daughter, then she shall live. (Exo 1:15-16)*

This is the introduction to the book of Exodus, and as we can see, it continues the story that began on page one of the Bible.

Food for thought

Verses 11-13 - There are strong verbal links between this chapter and Genesis 15:13, God's promise to Abraham. Notice "afflict", "afflicted", and "serve". This begins to show that the Exodus from Egypt was a fulfilment of the promise made to Abraham in Genesis 15.

Verse 19 - The midwives played on the fears of the Egyptians, who were so afraid of the Israelites that they were starting to think of them as a superior race (see verses 9 and 12).

Exodus 2

Moses: self-willed and angry

Moses is introduced in this chapter as the son of a Levite mother and a Levite father. The Bible is drawing attention to his lineage as a pure descendant of Levi. Levi is the third son of Leah, Jacob's first wife and the only one he buries in the family plot with Abraham and Sarah, Isaac and Rebekah:

> There they buried Abraham and Sarah his wife; there they buried Isaac and Rebekah his wife; and there I buried Leah. (Gen 49:31)

This verse tells us that Leah is counted as the one through whom God would pass the promises to Abraham and Isaac. Looking at the words of Jacob to his sons before he died (Genesis 49), we see that the words about Simeon and Levi are not wholly positive:

> Simeon and Levi are brethren; instruments of cruelty are in their habitations. O my soul, come not thou into their secret; unto their assembly, mine honour, be not thou united: for **in their anger they slew a man**, and in their selfwill they digged down a wall. Cursed be their anger, for it was fierce; and their wrath, for it was

cruel: I will divide them in Jacob, and scatter them in Israel. (Gen 49:5-7)

This fierce anger, and cruel wrath, is noted by Jacob as a trait the brothers possess. The scriptures are drawing our attention to it by calling Moses the son of two Levites. So is there anything in the life of Moses that suggests he had these character traits too?

And it came to pass in those days, when Moses was grown, that he went out unto his brethren, and looked on their burdens: and he spied an Egyptian smiting an Hebrew, one of his brethren. And he looked this way and that way, and when he saw that there was no man, **he slew the Egyptian***, and hid him in the sand. (Exo 2:11-12)*

It's extremely apt that this should be the case with Moses. The Bible appears to be telling us that the saga of Levi and his anger, is continuing through Moses. While we may see Moses in our mind's eye as the white-haired, white-bearded old man coming down from the mountain with the stone tables of the law, we should see that first of all he was just like Levi, allowing his anger to get the better of him.

In the years following, during his exile, Moses learns to temper his anger and self-will, so that later on during the exodus from Egypt, God says this of him:

(Now the man Moses was very meek, above all the men which were upon the face of the earth.) (Num 12:3)

Meekness is the total opposite of self-will and wrath. In our own journey through life, we can hope that our natural character can, over time, be changed so drastically that it is no longer recognisable. Moses changed over that forty years, from a self-willed and hot-tempered youth, to a meek man who walked in the right way before God. This changed man is ultimately portrayed as the greatest of men, and a forerunner of Jesus himself:

> And there arose not a prophet since in Israel like unto Moses, whom the LORD knew face to face... (Deu 34:10)
>
> For Moses truly said unto the fathers, A prophet shall the Lord your God raise up unto you of your brethren, like unto me; him shall ye hear in all things whatsoever he shall say unto you. (Act 3:22)

Food for thought

Verse 10 - "The child grew" might seem to be a very obvious comment! However it passes into Biblical use in a very significant way, speaking of men who became faithful servants of God— Judges 13:24, 1 Samuel 2:21,26, Luke 1:80, 2:40—and it has its origins in Genesis 21:8.

Verse 22 - In saying "I have been a stranger in a strange land" Moses is reflecting on the promise that God made to Abraham in Genesis 15:13.

Exodus 3

The God of Abraham, Isaac and Jacob

It is interesting that Moses feels he needs a name for God, to distinguish Him from the gods of the Egyptians:

> And Moses said unto God, Behold, when I come unto the children of Israel, and shall say unto them, The God of your fathers hath sent me unto you; and they shall say to me, What is his name? what shall I say unto them? (Exo 3:13)

The answer is not what Moses expects, or perhaps what we would expect. God says, simply, "I am", and leaves it at that:

> And God said unto Moses, I AM THAT I AM: and he said, Thus shalt thou say unto the children of Israel, I AM hath sent me unto you. (Exo 3:14)

God is referring to the fact that He is the only God, and that it is rather incongruous to ask Him which god He is. Perhaps He is also drawing Moses's mind to the very first verse of the Bible, where He was there at the beginning. It is the way we are introduced to God:

In the beginning God... (Gen 1:1)

This Hebrew word "I am" is there in the second verse, translated as "was":

*And the earth **was** without form, and void; and darkness was upon the face of the deep. And the Spirit of God moved upon the face of the waters. (Gen 1:2)*

So I think God was drawing Abraham's attention to the fact that He was there at the beginning of creation, and has always been, and therefore needs no name to distinguish Him.

But then God says something interesting, and it is a very wonderful proof to us that God, as mighty and all powerful and ever living as He is, wishes to dwell with mankind and have us understand Him:

*And God said moreover unto Moses, Thus shalt thou say unto the children of Israel, **The LORD God of your fathers, the God of Abraham, the God of Isaac, and the God of Jacob**, hath sent me unto you: **this is my name for ever**, and this is my memorial unto all generations. Go, and gather the elders of Israel together, and say unto them, **The LORD God of your fathers, the God of Abraham, of Isaac, and of Jacob**, appeared unto me, saying, I have surely visited you, and seen that which is done to you in Egypt... (Exo 3:15-16)*

God tells Abraham that He wishes to be known as the God of Abraham, of Isaac, and of Jacob. In other words, He wishes the descendants of Jacob to understand that He is the God who gave the promises to Abraham, Isaac and Jacob, who changed Jacob's name to "Israel", and who promised that He was going to bring them out of the land of their captivity:

> *And he said unto Abram, Know of a surety that thy seed shall be a stranger in a land that is not theirs, and shall serve them; and they shall afflict them four hundred years; And also that nation, whom they shall serve, will I judge: and afterward shall they come out with great substance. (Gen 15:13-14)*

Jesus, in the new testament, quoted these words and confirmed that his God was the same God, and still known by that same name:

> *But as touching the resurrection of the dead, have ye not read that which was spoken unto you by God, saying, I am the God of Abraham, and the God of Isaac, and the God of Jacob? God is not the God of the dead, but of the living. (Mat 22:31-32)*

Jesus uses our chapter, and the incident of Moses at the burning bush, to declare that God will raise Abraham, Isaac and Jacob from the dead. It is impossible for them to stay in the grave, because:

> *this is My name **forever**.*

Food for thought

Verse 9 - The cry of people can come up to God in one of two different ways. On this occasion, God heard their cry and sought to deliver them. In Genesis 18:20-21 the cry of the people brought God's judgment upon Sodom and Gomorrah.

Verses 20-21 - God's assurance that Israel would leave Egypt "not empty" was a long time coming, or so it might seem from the time that they were made to serve Egypt. However, when Israel left Egypt, God's words were fulfilled completely (Exo 11:3, 12:36).

Exodus 4

Moses and Zipporah split up

Moses accepts all that God is telling him, even though it means his life will change drastically and never be the same again. Moses demonstrates faith like that of Abraham, Isaac and Jacob by accepting God's word at face value and believing it.

> *And Moses took his wife and his sons, and set them upon an ass, and he returned to the land of Egypt: and Moses took the rod of God in his hand. (Exo 4:20)*

But don't forget, this didn't only affect Moses, it affected his family too. Was his wife supposed to accept this change as easily as Moses did - even though she didn't see the signs or hear God's voice?

In Genesis we find several similar examples: two wives who went with their husbands, seemingly without question, and one who turned back. Sarah followed Abraham wherever he went, though it meant leaving her mother and father's family behind, and moving to a strange country. Rebekah likewise left her family, not knowing where she was going or what Isaac, her new husband, would be like. Lot's wife, on the other hand, needed to be taken by the hand and pulled away, yet yearned to go back. Her fate was to be turned into a pillar of salt:

> But his wife looked back from behind him, and she became a pillar of salt. (Gen 19:26)

Zipporah struggled with Moses's sudden departure. She was only very distantly related to the people of Israel, being a descendant of Midian, Abraham's son by Keturah; and perhaps she didn't have the same drive to go and rescue Israel from Egypt. It is a testament to her faithfulness as a wife that she agreed to come with Moses at all, leaving behind everything she had ever known, and setting off into unknown territory with only the stuff she could carry, and with their young children in tow. Was Moses perhaps asking too much of her? After all, God asked *Moses* to go, not his wife and children.

And then disaster strikes on the way:

> And it came to pass by the way in the inn, that the LORD met him, and sought to kill him. Then Zipporah took a sharp stone, and cut off the foreskin of her son, and cast it at his feet, and said, Surely a bloody husband art thou to me. So he let him go: then she said, A bloody husband thou art, because of the circumcision. (Exo 4:24-26)

The incident regarding circumcision shows us that Zipporah had not yet accepted circumcision, the bond of the covenant between God and Abraham, which meant that she had not fully accepted Moses' God or his people:

> And God said unto Abraham, Thou shalt keep my covenant therefore, thou, and thy seed after thee in their generations. This

> is my covenant, which ye shall keep, between me and you and thy seed after thee; Every man child among you shall be circumcised. (Gen 17:9-10)

This appears to have been a great source of contention in their marriage, as you can see from her words where she blames Moses:

> ... Surely a bloody husband art thou to me. (Exo 4:25)

At this stage it appears that Moses and Zipporah (and the children) parted company. She and the boys went home, and he went on. Perhaps they both agreed that this mission was too much to expect of her and the children - and in hindsight, knowing all we do about the Exodus, I think we would agree. So was this woman repeating the mistake that Lot's wife made?

I think not. I think it is more likely that we simply have a story of the development of a character, probably much like the story of our own lives. It is not easy to accept the challenges to the status quo that faith in the God of Abraham, Isaac and Jacob puts on us. It takes us some time to adjust. The story has a happy ending, though, because Moses returned to the mountain near Midian where he had received God's words, and he and his wife and children were reunited there. In chapter 18 we see that her father brings her and her children out to Moses, having realised that the miraculous deliverance Moses spoke of those months earlier, had in fact occurred:

> When Jethro, the priest of Midian, Moses' father in law, heard of all that God had done for Moses, and for Israel his people, and that the LORD had brought Israel out of Egypt; then Jethro, Moses' father in law, took Zipporah, Moses' wife, after he had sent her back, ... And Jethro, Moses' father in law, came with his sons and

his wife unto Moses into the wilderness, where he encamped at the mount of God... (Exo 18:1-2, 5)

Food for thought

Verse 1 - Moses could be forgiven for thinking that Israel would not believe him because they did not believe that he was the deliverer when he slew the Egyptian forty years earlier (see Acts 7:25).

Verse 22 - This is the first time that Israel is presented as God's "firstborn", and from now on this language, and the idea that Israel is God's son, passes into Biblical use. So whenever we read of Israel as God's son we should think of the deliverance from Egypt. A typical passage which makes this point very clearly is Hosea 11:1.

Exodus 5

How many signs does it take to believe?

It is a little-known fact that the first plague, the turning of water into blood, was originally meant for the children of Israel. Note God's words to Moses at the burning bush:

> *And Moses answered and said, But, behold, they will not believe me, nor hearken unto my voice: for they will say, The LORD hath not appeared unto thee. ... And it shall come to pass, if they will not believe also these two signs, neither hearken unto thy voice, that thou shalt take of the water of the river, and pour it upon the dry land: and the water which thou takest out of the river shall become blood upon the dry land. (Exo 4:1, 9)*

This sign was reserved for "if they will not believe", referring to the elders of the children of Israel. It appears that this sign was not necessary, since it is recorded that they *did* believe:

> *And the people believed: and when they heard that the LORD had visited the children of Israel, and that he had looked upon their affliction, then they bowed their heads and worshipped. (Exo 4:31)*

So we have a great start to the work of Moses, in that the people believed and worshipped God. Belief (faith) in God is the basis of all good things that might come from Him:

> *But without faith it is impossible to please him: for he that cometh to God must believe that he is, and that he is a **rewarder** of them that diligently seek him.* (Heb 11:6)

Moses appears in that same chapter of Hebrews, as having understood this:

> *By faith Moses, when he was come to years, refused to be called the son of Pharaoh's daughter; choosing rather to suffer affliction with the people of God, than to enjoy the pleasures of sin for a season; esteeming the reproach of Christ greater riches than the treasures in Egypt: for **he had respect unto the recompence of the reward**.* (Heb 11:24-26)

So we have Moses and the people of Israel united in their faith in God, believing that He will save them. Pharaoh, however, still needs to be presented with the same evidence:

> *And Pharaoh said, Who is the LORD, that I should obey his voice to let Israel go? I know not the LORD, neither will I let Israel go.* (Exo 5:2)

He will undergo the same signs that persuaded Moses and the elders of Israel, yet still not believe. Pharaoh, whose heart was hardened, believed at the last, but only when it was too late:

> *And the Egyptians shall know that I am the LORD, when I have*

gotten me honour upon Pharaoh, upon his chariots, and upon his horsemen. (Exo 14:18)

Pharaoh and his cavalry finally knew that the LORD is God, when the waters of the sea closed in around them. We see in Pharaoh, the elders of Israel, and in Moses, a range of examples of how quickly we might accept God and believe in Him. Either we do so early, and benefit from His goodness, or we do so late, when we may be out of time.

Food for thought

Chapter note - Israel may have thought that if their exodus was a fulfilment of Genesis 15, then they ought to be let go easily. However, it is clear that God wished to manifest His might and power extensively and in so doing teach Israel His might and prepare them for greater things. Hence Pharaoh refuses to let Israel go at the first.

Verses 22-23 - Moses has been willing to go to Pharaoh, but because things are not going smoothly, he begins to question God. At this time Moses does not fully understand that the deliverance of Israel would be a consequence of the destruction of Egypt. Likewise our deliverance from sin has a cost. It is the destruction of sinful thoughts in ourselves (Galatians 5:24).

Exodus 6

No-one listened to Moses

Verses 14-25 are an interlude in the narrative, to highlight the family lineage of Moses and Aaron. You can see that verse 12 is repeated in verse 30 to show where the narrative takes up again. Why is this?

Within these verses we find that Moses and Aaron were from one of the chief families of Levi; in other words, they had authority bestowed on them by their lineage:

> ... these are the heads of the fathers of the Levites according to their families. These are that Aaron and Moses, to whom the LORD said, Bring out the children of Israel from the land of Egypt according to their armies. (Exo 6:25-26)

This appears to be further confirmed when we consider that another man in that lineage, Korah (see v21), Moses' cousin, was seen by the children of Israel as a possible alternative to Moses's leadership:

> Now Korah, the son of Izhar, the son of Kohath, the son of Levi... took men: and they rose up before Moses, with certain of the

> *children of Israel, two hundred and fifty princes of the assembly, famous in the congregation, men of renown: (Num 16:1-2)*

Thus when Moses complained to God that no-one had listened to him, it was perhaps on the basis that the people had not accepted his or Aaron's authority as given to them by their family status.

> *And Moses spake before the LORD, saying, Behold, the children of Israel have not hearkened unto me; how then shall Pharaoh hear me, who am of uncircumcised lips? (Exo 6:12)*

But that was missing the point. The point is that God had sent him! In the next verse after the interlude, we see that none of this mattered to God, because He would provide the authority by His signs and miracles, elevating Moses in Pharaoh's sight to be like a god:

> *And the LORD said unto Moses, See, I have made thee a god to Pharaoh: and Aaron thy brother shall be thy prophet. (Exo 7:1)*

Fulfilling the promises to Abraham

The language of this chapter draws heavily on the language of Genesis 17, in which God promises the land of Canaan to Abraham and his seed. God is showing that the return from Egypt is a fulfilment (though not the complete fulfilment) of some of the promises to Abraham.
    v.2 I am the LORD (Gen 15:7)
    v.3 God Almighty (Gen 17:1)
    v.4 established my covenant (Gen 17:7)
    v.4 the land of Canaan (Gen 17:8)
    v.4 land … strangers (Gen 17:8)
    v.8 I am the LORD (Gen 15:7)

Food for thought

Verse 8 - In speaking of the land which was sworn to Abraham, Isaac and Jacob, God is actually quoting the words of Joseph to Moses as an evidence that He is going to keep His word (Gen 50:24).

Verses 12, 30 - In saying "I am of uncircumcised lips" Moses is making rather a lame excuse, it seems. God had called him to do the work and so he should have simply got on with it. Easy as it is to say this, we need to realise that we are often just like Moses.

Exodus 7

Respect for those we disagree with

Have you noticed the phrase in verse 1: "I have made thee a god to Pharaoh"?

> *And the LORD said unto Moses, See, I have made thee a god to Pharaoh: and Aaron thy brother shall be thy prophet. (Exo 7:1)*

Similarly with Joseph:

> *So now it was not you that sent me hither, but God: and he hath made me a father to Pharaoh, and lord of all his house, and a ruler throughout all the land of Egypt. (Gen 45:8)*

God is able to bring His servants into a position of respect, or even awe, before rulers. But notice Moses' example in all his dealings with Pharaoh. Even though he doesn't agree with the man, he is respectful, gracious, and willing to aid Pharaoh when asked:

> *Then Pharaoh called for Moses and Aaron, and said, "Entreat the*

LORD that He may take away the frogs from me and from my people; and I will let the people go, that they may sacrifice to the LORD." And Moses said to Pharaoh, "Accept the honor of saying when I shall intercede for you, for your servants, and for your people, to destroy the frogs from you and your houses, that they may remain in the river only." So he said, "Tomorrow." And he said, "Let it be according to your word, that you may know that there is no one like the LORD our God. (Exo 8:8-10 NKJV)

We are told that these words were given to him by God Himself:

Thou shalt speak all that I command thee: and Aaron thy brother shall speak unto Pharaoh, that he send the children of Israel out of his land. (Exo 7:2)

This would in the future be exemplified by the apostles after Jesus was risen, who spoke before rulers to present to them the gospel:

But take heed to yourselves: for they shall deliver you up to councils; and in the synagogues ye shall be beaten: and ye shall be brought before rulers and kings for my sake, for a testimony against them. And the gospel must first be published among all nations. But when they shall lead you, and deliver you up, take no thought beforehand what ye shall speak, neither do ye premeditate: but whatsoever shall be given you in that hour, that speak ye: for it is not ye that speak, but the Holy [Spirit]. (Mar 13:9-11)

Food for thought

Verse 2 - When God tells Moses that "Thou shalt speak all that I command thee", God is not only telling Moses that he will not have to work out for himself what he should say to Pharaoh. In God's foreknowledge, He is also describing the role of Jesus, the prophet like Moses, as described in Deuteronomy 18:18.

Verse 7 - Just a little point, but this verse demonstrates that Aaron was three years older than Moses. We should be alert to the incidental details we can pick up from the text, which provide information that will be of general value.

Exodus 8

Hear him!

The plagues are designed to show Pharaoh that Moses has the authority to speak on God's behalf. Take a look back at God's original meeting with Moses, where it shows us this:

> And Moses answered and said, But, behold, they will not believe me, nor **hearken unto my voice:** for they will say, The LORD hath not appeared unto thee ... And it shall come to pass, if they will not believe also these two signs, neither **hearken unto thy voice**, that thou shalt take of the water of the river, and pour it upon the dry land: and the water which thou takest out of the river shall become blood upon the dry land. (Exo 4:1, 9)

This proves that the plagues were so that the people would believe Moses, hearken to his voice, and believe that the LORD had appeared to him. We see this in action, because this plague of blood is then carried out in front of Pharaoh:

> And Moses and Aaron did so, as the LORD commanded; and he lifted up the rod, and smote the waters that were in the river, in

the sight of Pharaoh, and in the sight of his servants; and all the waters that were in the river were turned to blood. (Exo 7:20)

So Moses is God's mouthpiece. Now notice in our current chapter that while Moses delivers God's ultimatum, he does not wait for an answer:

And the LORD spake unto Moses, Go unto Pharaoh, and say unto him, Thus saith the LORD, Let my people go, that they may serve me. And if thou refuse to let them go, behold, I will smite all thy borders with frogs ... And Aaron stretched out his hand over the waters of Egypt; and the frogs came up, and covered the land of Egypt. (Exo 8:1-2, 6)

Presumably there was some time given to Pharaoh to answer Moses, but he simply ignored it and didn't answer. The ultimatum was delivered, and he took no action.

So in the next plague, the LORD God does it without warning Pharaoh any further:

But when Pharaoh saw that there was respite, he hardened his heart, and hearkened not unto them; as the LORD had said. And the LORD said unto Moses, Say unto Aaron, Stretch out thy rod, and smite the dust of the land, that it may become lice throughout all the land of Egypt. (Exo 8:15-16)

Each time it is Moses who lifts the plague, by entreating the LORD in prayer:

And Moses and Aaron went out from Pharaoh: and Moses cried unto the LORD because of the frogs which he had brought against Pharaoh. And the LORD did according to the word of Moses; and the frogs died out of the houses, out of the villages, and out of the fields. (Exo 8:12-13)

So we see that Moses was made by God a mediator between the LORD and man. Moses spoke the message God had given Him, caused the plagues to come, was the one to whom confession was made, and then entreated the LORD for the removal of each plague once he was asked to do so by Pharaoh. In other words, Pharaoh had a direct line of communication to the LORD God through Moses.

We also have a direct line of communication to God through the Lord Jesus. His miracles similarly proved that he was sent by God and had been given by God. The LORD God's specific message about Jesus, given from heaven, was to hear him:

And there came a voice out of the cloud, saying, This is my beloved Son: **hear him.** *(Luk 9:35)*

And by this He proclaimed that Jesus was the one, like Moses, whom they were waiting for:

I will raise them up a Prophet from among their brethren, like unto [Moses], and will put my words in his mouth; and he shall speak unto them all that I shall command him. And it shall come to pass, that whosoever will not hearken unto my words which he shall speak in my name, I will require it of him. (Deu 18:18-19)

The result of the people not listening to Jesus, the one like Moses, was that the destruction of AD70 came upon them, resulting in two millennia of scattering and persecution.

Food for thought

Verse 19 - The magicians assert that Moses' miracles are done by "the finger of God". Jesus, when being accused of casting out devils by Beelzebub, asserts that he is casting out devils by the finger of God, saying: "But if I with the finger of God cast out devils, no doubt the kingdom of God is come upon you" (Luke 11:20). He is showing them that the magicians in Egypt were more perceptive than the Jews who were questioning his authority in performing miracles.

Verse 23 - Part way through the plagues God "put a division between" Israel and the Egyptians. So we should ask: "Why did God bring some of the plagues upon His own people?" The answer is that Israel were rebellious in the land of Egypt and had refused to listen to one of God's prophets - probably Moses - and so were being punished (Ezekiel 20:6-8)

Exodus 9

Unto every one that hath, shall be given

Abraham, Isaac, Jacob and Joseph all spent time as refugees in other lands. Yet while living there, God blessed them and made a distinction between them and the other inhabitants. Take for example Jacob and Laban:

> *And the man [Jacob] increased exceedingly, and had much cattle, and maidservants, and menservants, and camels, and asses ... And he heard the words of Laban's sons, saying, Jacob hath taken away all that was our father's; and of that which was our father's hath he gotten all this glory. (Gen 30:43 - 31:1)*

In each case they came out with more than they went in with. It's the same in this chapter:

> *And the LORD shall sever between the cattle of Israel and the cattle of Egypt: and there shall nothing die of all that is the children's of Israel ... and all the cattle of Egypt died: but of the cattle of the children of Israel died not one. (Exo 9:4, 6)*

Egypt ends up with less, and Israel more. What lesson is God teaching us with these examples?

In the New Testament Jesus tells a parable where one man has something taken away and given to another. Perhaps Jesus is looking back at Abraham, Isaac and Israel to form the basis of his teaching?

> *Take therefore the talent from him, and give it unto him which hath ten talents. For unto every one that hath shall be given, and he shall have abundance: but from him that hath not shall be taken away even that which he hath. (Mat 25:28-29)*

Jesus' conclusion fits completely the plagues of Egypt, because what started with God making a distinction between Egypt and Israel, ended with Him taking what little they had left, and giving it to His people:

> *And the LORD gave the people favour in the sight of the Egyptians, so that they lent unto them such things as they required. And they spoiled the Egyptians. (Exo 12:36)*

Food for thought

Verse 18 - The "very grievous hail" that fell on Egypt was really out of keeping with Egyptian experience. Egypt does not have rain, as Zechariah informs us (Zec 14:18) - so the Egyptians should really have seen God was at work, especially as they had suffered so many other things at the hand of God. However, they probably were able to rationalise the event as a natural disaster - though quite an unusual one. It is so easy for man to dismiss Gods involvement in world affairs as chance happenings, or provide explanations as to why they have happened. This is a very foolish way of thinking, and there is a danger that we might think similarly and fail to recognise that God is working in our lives.

Verse 34 - This is the first time that we are told that Pharaoh's servants' hearts were hardened. So the obstinate mind of Pharaoh caused his servants to be of the same mind. It is so easy to hold a view because others influence our viewpoint. We should be sure in our own minds what is correct. In the case of Pharaoh's servants, they had seen his behaviour a number of times on this matter, and eventually they join him. Likewise we might manage to resist the inclination to be 'led' for a while, but if we continue in the same company eventually we will fall - be careful what company you keep!

Exodus 10

Did Egypt survive the plagues?

After seven plagues on the land, how much food or cattle do you think were left?

> *And Pharaoh's servants said unto him, How long shall this man be a snare unto us? let the men go, that they may serve the LORD their God: knowest thou not yet that Egypt is destroyed? (Exo 10:7)*

Pharaohs officials tell him, "do you not yet know that Egypt is destroyed?" And when the locusts came to eat up the rest, Pharaoh himself knew that this plague, if left to continue, would bring about the starvation of every one of them:

> *Then Pharaoh called for Moses and Aaron in haste; and he said, I have sinned against the LORD your God, and against you. Now therefore forgive, I pray thee, my sin only this once, and intreat the LORD your God, **that He may take away from me this death only**. (Exo 10:16-17)*

But it was not God's intention to destroy Egypt, or He could have done it, as with the city of Sodom. His purpose was to show His strength to Israel and Egypt for generations to come:

> *And the LORD said unto Moses, Go in unto Pharaoh: for I have hardened his heart, and the heart of his servants, that I might shew these my signs before him: And that thou mayest tell in the ears of thy son, and of thy son's son, what things I have wrought in Egypt, and my signs which I have done among them; that ye may know how that I am the LORD. (Exo 10:1-2)*

As you read through your Bible this year, consider how often God refers back to these words. This is one of the statements that frame the rest of Israel's history right up to the death of Stephen in Acts 7:36-39.

Food for thought

Verses 1,7 - It seems that, whilst Pharaoh's heart and his servants hearts were "hardened", the servants were not as belligerent as Pharaoh. But there was something else at work here. God wanted to show His power to the rest of the world – Exo 9:16.

Verse 2 - Teaching the sons, and son's sons, actually becomes a feature of how God wants Israel to teach His laws. See for example Deuteronomy 4:9.

Exodus 11

An early warning. Action too late.

Moses left Pharaoh in great anger. What was the reason for this anger?

> *And all these thy servants shall come down unto me, and bow down themselves unto me, saying, Get thee out, and all the people that follow thee: and after that I will go out. And he went out from Pharaoh in a great anger. (Exo 11:8)*

Moses saw that Pharaoh's servants believed in God, and yet Pharaoh didn't listen to their concerns. The people knew, now, that God would make good on His promise to carry out this last, and most terrible, plague. In fact, they had done so for quite some time, and had noticed that God kept their neighbours safe from these plagues. This explains how in the midst of all this carnage they held Moses and the people of Israel in such awe:

> *Speak now in the ears of the people, and let every man borrow of his neighbour, and every woman of her neighbour, jewels of silver, and jewels of gold. And the LORD gave the people favour in the*

sight of the Egyptians. Moreover the man Moses was very great in the land of Egypt, in the sight of Pharaoh's servants, and in the sight of the people. (Exo 11:2-3)

And yet these things had been prophesied from the first day. God had already said what He was going to do, and each plague had been proof, and more proof, that He would do as He said:

And the LORD said unto Moses, When thou goest to return into Egypt, see that thou do all those wonders before Pharaoh, which I have put in thine hand: but I will harden his heart, that he shall not let the people go. And thou shalt say unto Pharaoh, Thus saith the LORD, Israel is my son, even my firstborn: And I say unto thee, Let my son go, that he may serve me: and if thou refuse to let him go, behold, I will slay thy son, even thy firstborn. (Exo 4:21-23)

It would have been well for Pharaoh and the people to listen to Moses at the outset.

But some people did. Some of the Egyptians did listen, and we know this because when the call came to leave Egypt, they went too:

And a mixed multitude went up also with them; and flocks, and herds, even very much cattle. (Exo 12:38)

The idea of serving God early is one well worth considering. God rises up early to warn us:

And the LORD said unto Moses, Rise up early in the morning, and stand before Pharaoh... (Exo 8:20)

And the LORD said unto Moses, Rise up early in the morning, and stand before Pharaoh... (Exo 9:13)

I have sent also unto you all my servants the prophets, rising up early and sending them... (Jer 35:15)

And He loves those who do not leave it too late to respond:

I love them that love me; and those that seek me early shall find me. (Pro 8:17)

Food for thought

Verse 8 - How do we think Moses' anger fits into his being "meek" (Num 12:3)?

Verse 10 - The words "all these wonders", spoken before the final plague, must mean that the point being made is that everything that has happened up to now forms part of the wonderful evidence that God provided to Israel – and to the nations who heard of these things, as did the men of Jericho (Josh 2:10).

Exodus 12

The armies of the LORD

Have you noticed in this chapter that God calls the people of Israel an army?

*And ye shall observe the feast of unleavened bread; for in this selfsame day have I brought **your armies** out of the land of Egypt: therefore shall ye observe this day in your generations by an ordinance for ever ... And it came to pass at the end of the four hundred and thirty years, even the selfsame day it came to pass, that **all the hosts of the LORD** went out from the land of Egypt ... And it came to pass the selfsame day, that the LORD did bring the children of Israel out of the land of Egypt by **their armies**.* (Exo 12:17, 41, 51)

This explains to us the primary purpose of Jacob's family going into Egypt. They had been dwelling in a land that had been promised to them, but they didn't have the numbers to populate it. So we see Abraham, Isaac and Jacob dwelling amongst other people even though the land had been promised to them. God's purpose in sending them to Egypt is primarily to make them into an army of people, capable occupying the whole land of Canaan and casting out the wicked people who lived there:

> *And he said unto Abram, Know of a surety that thy seed shall be a stranger in a land that is not theirs, and shall serve them; and they shall afflict them four hundred years; And also that nation, whom they shall serve, will I judge: and afterward shall they **come out with great substance**... But in the fourth generation they shall come hither again: **for the iniquity of the Amorites is not yet full**. (Gen 15:13-16)*

Staying in the house of Jesus

God was going to smite Egypt with a final plague, and the children of Israel could avoid this plague by putting the blood of a lamb on the lintel and doorposts of the door to their house:

> *And they shall take of the blood, and strike it on the two side posts and on the upper door post of the houses, wherein they shall eat it ... And the blood shall be to you for a token upon the houses where ye are: and when I see the blood, I will pass over you, and the plague shall not be upon you to destroy you, when I smite the land of Egypt. (Exo 12:7, 13)*

This observance gave name to the feast of "passover", which was to be kept every year thereafter:

> *And ye shall observe this thing for an ordinance to thee and to thy sons for ever. And it shall come to pass, when ye be come to the land which the LORD will give you, according as he hath promised, that ye shall keep this service. (Exo 12:24-25)*

The reason for this observance year by year was to safeguard the lesson of this deliverance and pass it on from generation to generation:

> And it shall come to pass, when your children shall say unto you, What mean ye by this service? That ye shall say, It is the sacrifice of the LORD'S passover, who passed over the houses of the children of Israel in Egypt, when he smote the Egyptians, and delivered our houses. And the people bowed the head and worshipped. (Exo 12:26-27)

The point that is made strongly here is that one could be saved by remaining in the house, through the blood of the lamb. We too, by remaining in the household of Christ, can be saved by his blood:

> Forasmuch as ye know that ye were not redeemed with corruptible things, as silver and gold, from your vain conversation received by tradition from your fathers; But with the precious blood of Christ, as of a lamb without blemish and without spot... (1Pe 1:18-19)

> And Moses verily was faithful in all his house, as a servant, for a testimony of those things which were to be spoken after; but Christ as a son over his own house; whose house are we, if we hold fast the confidence and the rejoicing of the hope firm unto the end. (Heb 3:5-6)

Food for thought

Verse 2 - The Jewish civil and religious calendars are adrift by 6 months. The day of atonement in the seventh month marks the beginning of the secular year, whilst Passover marks the beginning of the religious year.

Verse 25 - "when ye be come into the land" provided Israel with an assurance as to where they were going even before they left Egypt. Their departure was not to some unknown destination and an uncertain future.

Exodus 13

Through faith he kept the Passover

The book of Genesis ended with Joseph giving commandment that his bones should be taken with the children of Israel when God delivered them:

> *And Joseph said unto his brethren, I die: and God will surely visit you, and bring you out of this land unto the land which he sware to Abraham, to Isaac, and to Jacob. And Joseph took an oath of the children of Israel, saying, God will surely visit you, and ye shall carry up my bones from hence.* (Gen 50:24-25)

This he did by faith in the promises to Abraham:

> *And [God] said unto Abram, Know of a surety that thy seed shall be a stranger in a land that is not theirs, and shall serve them; and they shall afflict them four hundred years; and also that nation, whom they shall serve, will I judge: and afterward shall they come out with great substance.* (Gen 15:13-14)

In the New Testament, he is specifically mentioned for this act of faith, which is to be an example to us:

> *By faith Joseph, when he died, made mention of the departing of the children of Israel; and gave commandment concerning his bones. (Heb 11:22)*

I wonder whether we would have chosen this particular aspect of Joseph's life to commend him for?

And what about Moses? What particular act of his faith would we mention in Hebrews 11, if it were up to us? Of the several entries Moses has, this same episode is also mentioned for him:

> *Through faith he kept the passover, and the sprinkling of blood, lest he that destroyed the firstborn should touch them. (Heb 11:28)*

The departure from Egypt clearly was a defining moment in the lives of many faithful men and women. Joseph and Moses, by being prepared for it before time, demonstrated that they believed (had faith in) God — that He was able to save them:

> *Now faith is the substance of things hoped for, the evidence of things not seen. (Heb 11:1)*

For us, living in the 21st century, our faith needs to be similar to this. God has told us that one day He will send His angels and gather the elect. What are we doing to prepare for that day?

> *For yourselves know perfectly that the day of the Lord so cometh as a thief in the night. For when they shall say, Peace and safety; then sudden destruction cometh upon them, as travail upon a woman with child; and they shall not escape. But ye, brethren, are not in*

darkness, that that day should overtake you as a thief. Ye are all the children of light, and the children of the day: we are not of the night, nor of darkness. Therefore let us not sleep, as do others; but let us watch and be sober. (1Th 5:2-6)

Food for thought

Verse 2 - The call to sanctify the firstborn was because God had killed the firstborn of all in Egypt. God had "bought" the firstborn in Israel as part of the deliverance from Egypt. In like manner we are "bought" by the death of a firstborn – 1Cor 6:20.

Verse 10 - Israel were to keep the Passover on the night that the Egyptians' firstborn were killed. However, it is made clear here that the Passover was to be kept every year thereafter. The annual feast was to remind them of their deliverance. Once in their own land it would have been so easy to forget the terrible bondage that Egypt brought upon the children of Israel, and the marvellous deliverance by God. We must take care that we do not lapse into forgetting the deliverance from sin and death achieved by the death and resurrection of Jesus. Thus Jesus instituted the "last supper" and asked that we remember him (Luk 22:19.

Exodus 14

A name for the LORD

In this chapter we see the culmination of God's purpose with the plagues in Egypt. Both the Egyptians and Israel ended up taking the name of the LORD on their lips:

> And [He] took off their chariot wheels, that they drave them heavily: so that the Egyptians said, Let us flee from the face of Israel; **for the LORD fighteth for them against the Egyptians** ... And Israel saw that great work which the LORD did upon the Egyptians: and **the people feared the LORD, and believed the LORD**, and his servant Moses. (Exo 14:25, 31)

In this chapter we are told clearly that this was the purpose of God for the Egyptians in their destruction:

> And I will harden Pharaoh's heart, that he shall follow after them; and **I will be honoured upon Pharaoh, and upon all his host; that the Egyptians may know that I am the LORD.** And they did so ... And I, behold, I will harden the hearts of the Egyptians, and they shall follow them: and I will get me honour upon Pharaoh,

*and upon all his host, upon his chariots, and upon his horsemen. And **the Egyptians shall know that I am the LORD**, when I have gotten me honour upon Pharaoh, upon his chariots, and upon his horsemen. (Exo 14:4, 17-18)*

The chapter is equally clear about God's purpose for the Jews in this event:

*But the children of Israel walked upon dry land in the midst of the sea; and the waters were a wall unto them on their right hand, and on their left. Thus the LORD saved Israel that day out of the hand of the Egyptians; and Israel saw the Egyptians dead upon the sea shore. And **Israel saw that great work which the LORD did** upon the Egyptians: and **the people feared the LORD, and believed the LORD**, and his servant Moses. (Exo 14:29-31)*

This dual effect of God's actions demonstrated to all people the character of God, making His Name distinct from the plethora of gods of the nations. This effect was permanent, far outlasting that generation:

*... and didst see the affliction of our fathers in Egypt, and heardest their cry by the Red sea; and shewedst signs and wonders upon Pharaoh, and on all his servants, and on all the people of his land: for thou knewest that they dealt proudly against them. **So didst thou get thee a name, as it is this day.** And thou didst divide the sea before them, so that they went through the midst of the sea on the dry land; and their persecutors thou threwest into the deeps, as a stone into the mighty waters. (Neh 9:9-11)*

Where did Israel cross the red sea?

We are told that Israel crossed the sea, but which sea was it, and where? In the next chapter we are told it was the Red Sea:

> *Pharaoh's chariots and his host hath he cast into the sea: his chosen captains also are drowned in the Red sea. (Exo 15:4)*

We are told in the book of Kings that the tip of the Gulf of Aqaba is the Red Sea:

> *And king Solomon made a navy of ships in Eziongeber, which is beside Eloth, on the shore of the Red sea, in the land of Edom. (1Ki 9:26)*

So it seems likely that Israel crossed over the gulf of Aqaba from within the Sinai peninsula into what is now Jordan or Saudi Arabia. There are many reasons for thinking this is likely. For example, it would make sense of the verse:

> *Then the dukes of Edom shall be amazed; the mighty men of Moab, trembling shall take hold upon them. (Exo 15:15)*

…because Moab and Edom are at the tip of the Gulf of Aqaba. It would also explain God's statement about Pharaoh's thoughts "the wilderness hath shut them in", if it meant the Sinai peninsula by the coast of the Gulf:

> *And the LORD spake unto Moses, saying, Speak unto the children of Israel, that they turn and encamp before Pihahiroth, between Migdol and the sea, over against Baalzephon: before it shall ye*

*encamp by the sea. For Pharaoh will say of the children of Israel, They are entangled in the land, **the wilderness hath shut them in**.* (Exo 14:1-3)

This deliberate act of turning from the main road (possibly the same as the current Taba - Nekhel Road[1]) into the dead-end wilderness was designed by God to entice Pharaoh to send his army out:

And I will harden Pharaoh's heart, that he shall follow after them; and I will be honoured upon Pharaoh, and upon all his host; that the Egyptians may know that I am the LORD. And they did so. (Exo 14:4)

All this was for the reason that God would be exalted in the sight of all nations when He delivered His people from harm, so that even now, thousands of years later, we might understand and have faith that "His mercy endures forever":

To him which divided the Red sea into parts: for his mercy endureth for ever: and made Israel to pass through the midst of it: for his mercy endureth for ever: but overthrew Pharaoh and his host in the Red sea: for his mercy endureth for ever. (Psa 136:13-15)

---

[1] Note: It had to be a main road because Pharaoh's war chariots were able to pass over it, and also his army were able to march there, see Exodus 15:7-9.

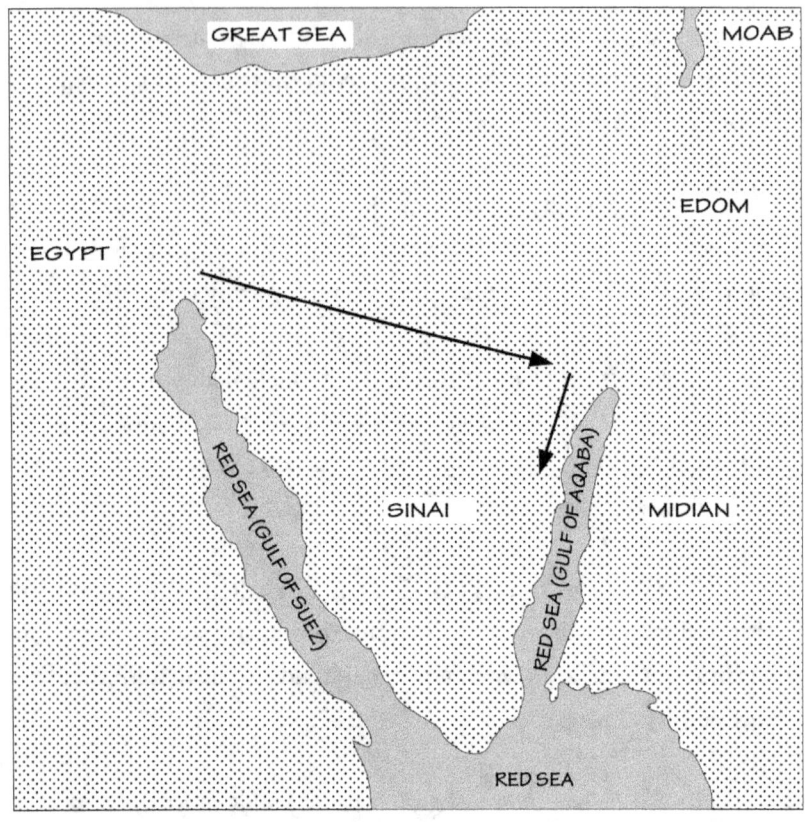

Food for thought

Note - Look closely at the comment in Hebrews 11:28-29 and you will see that Moses believed God with respect to the slaying of the firstborn, and by implication the nation did not, whereas by the time they passed through the Red Sea the nation believed that God was their deliverer.

Verse 13 - The call to "stand still and see the salvation of God" forms the basis for the exhortation to encourage Jehoshaphat (2Chron 20:17).

Exodus 15

Sweet victory and bitter shame

The victory was finally won!

> Then sang Moses and the children of Israel this song unto the LORD, and spake, saying, I will sing unto the LORD, for he hath triumphed gloriously: the horse and his rider hath he thrown into the sea. The LORD is my strength and song, and he is become my salvation: he is my God, and I will prepare him an habitation; my father's God, and I will exalt him. (Exo 15:1-2)

And now we would expect the children of Israel to be basking in that victory, of their release from slavery, and in their new freedom. But that was not to be:

> So Moses brought Israel from the Red sea, and they went out into the wilderness of Shur; and they went three days in the wilderness, and found no water. And when they came to Marah, they could not drink of the waters of Marah, for they were bitter: therefore the name of it was called Marah. And the people murmured against

FOOD FOR THOUGHT IN EXODUS

Moses, saying, What shall we drink? (Exo 15:22-24)

There are few more stark contrasts in scripture than this chapter, where people spontaneously express hope and joy, song and dance, then come crashing down to earth with a bang. Those sweet-tasting words of the song of deliverance changed to bitter complaints as they forgot God's power to save in the space of just three days.

Yet this type of contrast may be our daily experience. Whilst we might set more store in the high points in life, it is often the relative lows that God works with. So in this chapter, for example, the seed of faith in God was sown when Israel saw the mighty works. But this seed of faith still had to germinate and pop its head up into the light to see any real growth. And that growth would have to be steady, regular growth. This process started immediately when they realised over the next three days they had no water. They had to learn that trusting in God is a daily thing, not just for the big occasions.

Like the farmer who waits for the growth of his seed, what they had to learn was patience, to trust that God had everything under control. Had they waited a little longer before grumbling, they would have arrived at a rest stop tailor-made for them, with a watering place for each of the twelve tribes:

> *And they came to Elim, where were twelve wells of water, and threescore and ten palm trees: and they encamped there by the waters. (Exo 15:27)*

Our faith in God is shown by patience. God provides for those who put their trust in Him, and often the way that this faith is tried is by having to wait. It seems incongruous to us that the children of Israel waited a lifetime for deliverance from Egypt, and then could not wait three days' journey for water; yet if we are honest, how often is this kind of contradiction the same with us too?

> **Be patient** *therefore, brethren, unto the coming of the Lord. Behold, the husbandman waiteth for the precious fruit of the earth, and hath long patience for it, until he receive the early and latter rain.* **Be ye also patient;** *stablish your hearts: for the coming of the Lord draweth nigh. (Jas 5:7-8)*

Food for thought

Verse 2 - "The LORD is my strength and song, and he is become my salvation" is quoted by David (Psa 118:14), and Isaiah (Isa 12:2), and is echoed by Habakkuk in a song in which he reflects upon these events (Hab 3:18-19).

Verse 17 - In speaking of planting Israel, we see the beginning of a theme which runs through the prophets. In Psalm 80:8,15 the vine out of Egypt was planted. In Isaiah 5:2 a vine is planted. In Jeremiah 2:21 "I planted thee". Planting then passes into New Testament usage to speak of us, for example Romans 6:5 "planted together" and Ephesians 3:17 "rooted and grounded in love".

Exodus 16

"That I may prove them"

We're not told in this chapter whether the children of Israel ate the quails, even though they're mentioned here:

> *I have heard the murmurings of the children of Israel: speak unto them, saying, At even ye shall eat flesh, and in the morning ye shall be filled with bread; and ye shall know that I am the LORD your God. And it came to pass, that at even the quails came up, and covered the camp: and in the morning the dew lay round about the host. (Exo 16:12-13)*

Perhaps they were satisfied with the manna? There is more detail about the quails in Numbers, but that appears to be a later occasion:

> *And there went forth a wind from the LORD, and brought quails from the sea, and let them fall by the camp, as it were a day's journey on this side, and as it were a day's journey on the other side, round about the camp, and as it were two cubits high upon the face of the earth. (Num 11:31)*

Notice the difference between the two occasions. In the first, there is barely a mention of the quails, and in the second, perhaps much later in the journey, it was like an orgy of meat.

But notice also the reason God gives for sending them this abundant food to eat:

> *Then said the LORD unto Moses, Behold, I will rain bread from heaven for you; and **the people shall go out and gather a certain rate every day, that I may prove them**, whether they will walk in my law, or no. (Exo 16:4)*

God did this to "prove them". It seems that on this first occasion they acted with restraint and gathered only what was necessary for that day. On the second occasion, however, in their desperation for meat, they disobeyed this commandment:

> *And the people stood up all that day, and all that night, and all the next day, and they gathered the quails: he that gathered least gathered ten homers: and they spread them all abroad for themselves round about the camp. (Num 11:32)*

How much is ten homers? According to Strong's concordance a homer is about 300 litres, so this is saying each person gathered a minimum of 3000 litres volume of birds. A normal household bath holds about 200 litres, so if you imagine fifteen baths full of birds, that is how much each and every person gathered on that one occasion.

Do you know what I think? I think they didn't stop until they had killed **the entire flock of birds**.

This kind of craving is understandable, yet totally unacceptable for the follower of Christ. God has said that He will give us a portion of food every day, and that is what we should believe. If we lust for something, then God is willing to give to us in order to satisfy our cravings, but this has to be within the boundaries of decency. The way that they did it the first time was acceptable (they gathered enough) and the second time was indecent (they gathered it all, not believing that God could provide for the next day). The record confirms that their inner motivation was lust:

> *And the mixt multitude that was among them fell a lusting: and the children of Israel also wept again, and said, Who shall give us flesh to eat? (Num 11:4)*

For us, food may not be the thing we lust after. King David is an example of someone who had plenty, and yet lusted for what he didn't have. He sent his servant and took Bathsheba, a beautiful woman, but another man's wife. In God's rebuke, He tells David that if what he already had wasn't enough, he should have asked God for more, rather than giving in to his lust and taking what he wanted:

> *And I gave thee thy master's house, and thy master's wives into thy bosom, and gave thee the house of Israel and of Judah; and if that had been too little, I would moreover have given unto thee such and such things. (2Sa 12:8)*

Let us therefore have balance in our seeking after the things we lust for. Lust is natural, whether it is for food, or for beautiful women, or whatever else it may be. Lust is not something we can necessarily control. The answer, as God said to David, is to focus on what we do have, and to be thankful for it. If we still have need, we should pray to God rather than taking what is not ours. It may take patience, but in

God's good time He will provide what we need.

> *For every one that asketh receiveth; and he that seeketh findeth; and to him that knocketh it shall be opened. Or what man is there of you, whom if his son ask bread, will he give him a stone? Or if he ask a fish, will he give him a serpent? If ye then, being evil, know how to give good gifts unto your children, how much more shall your Father which is in heaven give good things to them that ask him? (Mat 7:8-11)*

Food for thought

Verse 3 - We should realise that Israel did not suffer hunger in the wilderness by accident or oversight on God's part. He caused them to suffer hunger - Deut 8:3 - that they might learn.

Verse 30 - So there was a law of the Sabbath before the law of Moses specified it a short while later. Here is one of the many indications that the Law of Moses was not the first time that God had laid down laws for His people to follow. Of course the first was "of all the trees ..." (Gen 2:16-17).

Exodus 17

"Is the LORD among us, or not?"

In the previous chapter God provided twelve wells of water, then miraculously provided quail and manna to eat. It doesn't say how much later the events in this chapter are, but once again the people forget God's ability to save them:

> And all the congregation of the children of Israel journeyed from the wilderness of Sin, after their journeys, according to the commandment of the LORD, and pitched in Rephidim: and there was no water for the people to drink. Wherefore the people did chide with Moses, and said, Give us water that we may drink. And Moses said unto them, Why chide ye with me? wherefore do ye tempt the LORD? (Exo 17:1-2)

This word "chide" is no longer commonly used, and if we look at the first time that this word is used in the Bible (Strongs number H7378) we can get a good idea of how sharp the contention was:

> And the herdmen of Gerar did **strive** with Isaac's herdmen, saying, The water is ours: and he called the name of the well Esek; because

> *they **strove** with him. (Gen 26:20)*

It is interesting that the scripture links these two passages together by using this word, because the context is the same too, of striving about water. How, then, did Isaac deal with it?

> *And they digged another well, and strove for that also: and he called the name of it Sitnah. And he removed from thence, and digged another well; and for that they strove not: and he called the name of it Rehoboth; and he said, For now the LORD hath made room for us, and we shall be fruitful in the land. (Gen 26:21-22)*

Incredibly, rather than continue to strive, Isaac simply moves on and digs another well. Then when that one doesn't work out, he moves and digs another one. At no point does it say that Isaac had a bad word to say against the herdsmen of Gerar. Isaac meekly accepted the setback, and trusted that the LORD would provide water for him, his household and his herds to drink.

Difficult as it is to do, this is to be our attitude too. Jesus advised us not to worry about what we will drink:

> *Therefore take no thought, saying, What shall we eat? or, What shall we drink? or, Wherewithal shall we be clothed? (For after all these things do the Gentiles seek:) for your heavenly Father knoweth that ye have need of all these things. (Mat 6:31-32)*

If God knows that we have need of these things, then for us to strive with Him and accuse Him of not providing is an act of tempting the LORD:

> *And he called the name of the place Massah, and Meribah, because*

> *of the chiding of the children of Israel, and because they tempted the LORD, saying, Is the LORD among us, or not? (Exo 17:7)*

But more than this, take a look at what the children of Israel were actually thinking as they strove with Moses:

> *And the people thirsted there for water; and the people murmured against Moses, and said, Wherefore is this that thou hast brought us up out of Egypt, to kill us and our children and our cattle with thirst? (Exo 17:3)*

In their thoughts, they actually blamed Moses (God's servant) of deliberately bringing them into the wilderness to kill them.

These things are easy to gloss over and perhaps we miss their significance. To accuse Moses, and, by implication, God, of seeking to kill you, is no small accusation. Imagine if you as a fireman risked your life to save a group of children from a burning school building, and then in the paper the next day you read that the children have said you set the fire and were trying to burn the school down on them?

These things are upsetting for the LORD, as they would be for us. The Psalmist says this of God's grief:

> *How oft did they provoke him in the wilderness, and grieve him in the desert! Yea, they turned back and tempted God, and limited the Holy One of Israel. (Psa 78:40-41)*

Let us not be like this, turning back in our hearts to Egypt. The New Testament speaks to us directly to implore us not to go the same way, and suffer the same fate, as the children of Israel. Let us instead take the example of Isaac and the advice of Jesus, who meekly trusted in the LORD God to provide their needs.

Wherefore I was grieved with that generation, and said, They do alway err in their heart; and they have not known my ways. So I sware in my wrath, They shall not enter into my rest. Take heed, brethren, lest there be in any of you an evil heart of unbelief, in departing from the living God. (Heb 3:10-12)

Food for thought

Verse 4 - That Moses had to cry to God because he did not know what to do about the absence of water teaches us that Moses was also being tested in the wilderness. However, he, unlike the rest of the people, realised that God would have the answer for him. Do we realise that God has all the answers for us in our "wilderness"?

Verse 14 - When Israel defeated Amalek, Moses was commanded to write down what God said about Amalek. This is the first occasion in Scripture we find a record of anyone being commanded to write down God's words.

Exodus 18

Sowing the seeds of rebellion

One of the things Moses learned during his 40 years in the wilderness of Midian as a shepherd was the ability to lead. We might think he had learned this at the feet of the best scholars and army generals in Egypt. But according to God, the qualifications for leadership are different from those in the world:

> *This is a true saying, If a man desire the office of a bishop, he desireth a good work. A bishop then must be blameless, the husband of one wife, vigilant, sober, of good behaviour, given to hospitality, apt to teach; not given to wine, no striker, not greedy of filthy lucre; but patient, not a brawler, not covetous; one that ruleth well his own house, having his children in subjection with all gravity; (for if a man know not how to rule his own house, how shall he take care of the church of God?) (1Ti 3:1-5)*

Here we have Paul's list of desired qualifications for leaders. Notice how they describe Moses perfectly. He was one who would recognise leadership quality in others, so why did Moses leave this judgement to his father-in-law to make? Jethro lists the qualifications of leadership, but notice how many attributes he leaves out:

> *Moreover thou shalt provide out of all the people able men, such as fear God, men of truth, hating covetousness; and place such over them, to be rulers of thousands, and rulers of hundreds, rulers of fifties, and rulers of tens. (Exo 18:21)*

And so, with this incomplete list of criteria, it was inevitable that some unsuitable leaders were chosen. The ramifications were that it led to a full rebellion against Moses. It appears that some of these men were swayed by the complaints that the people brought to them daily:

> *Now Korah, the son of Izhar, the son of Kohath, the son of Levi, and Dathan and Abiram, the sons of Eliab, and On, the son of Peleth, sons of Reuben, took men: and they rose up before Moses, with certain of the children of Israel, two hundred and fifty princes of the assembly, famous in the congregation, men of renown: and they gathered themselves together against Moses and against Aaron, and said unto them, Ye take too much upon you, seeing all the congregation are holy, every one of them, and the LORD is among them: wherefore then lift ye up yourselves above the congregation of the LORD? (Num 16:1-3)*

So was Moses right to listen to Jethro? Should he not also have enquired of God? When we hear advice do we check it against the Bible first before taking it?

Questions:

a) Compare Jethro's and Paul's list of qualifications for leadership. Which ones are missing in Jethro's list?

b) Which of these missing attributes could have helped avoid the leaders rebellion?

Food for thought

Verse 5 - Moses had clearly left Zipporah his wife when he returned to Egypt. Now within the first few months of the wilderness journey it would appear that Moses is reunited with Zipporah and his children. She would become the basis for complaints by Aaron and Miriam later, in Numbers 12:1.

Verses 13-18 - In these verses we gain an insight into Moses' dedication to the "church in the wilderness" (Acts 7:38). As such it gives us an indication of how we should care for our brothers and sisters – our fellow believers. Further, we should realise that those Moses helped were amongst the congregation who complained and murmured against God and Moses. Doubtless some of those who came to Moses were quite difficult individuals to deal with.

Exodus 19

Entering into the covenant

The children of Israel arrive at the mountain where God had first spoken to Moses from the burning bush:

> And Moses said unto God, Who am I, that I should go unto Pharaoh, and that I should bring forth the children of Israel out of Egypt? And he said, Certainly I will be with thee; and this shall be a token unto thee, that I have sent thee: When thou hast brought forth the people out of Egypt, **ye shall serve God upon this mountain**. (Exo 3:11-12)

And like that occasion, God speaks to him from the mountain:

> And Moses went up unto God, and the LORD called unto him out of the mountain, saying, Thus shalt thou say to the house of Jacob, and tell the children of Israel; Ye have seen what I did unto the Egyptians, and how I bare you on eagles' wings, and brought you unto myself. (Exo 19:3-4)

God is effectively saying, "look, I've done what I said I would do!"

The promise that God now gives to them is wonderful, but notice that it is dependant on their obedience:

> *Now therefore, if ye will obey my voice indeed, and keep my covenant, then ye shall be a peculiar treasure unto me above all people: for all the earth is mine: And ye shall be unto me a kingdom of priests, and an holy nation. These are the words which thou shalt speak unto the children of Israel. (Exo 19:5-6)*

The children of Israel accepted these terms, by answering as follows, and entering into a covenant with God:

> *And all the people answered together, and said,* **All that the LORD hath spoken we will do.** *And Moses returned the words of the people unto the LORD. (Exo 19:8)*

This is the covenant, or "testament", which gives the Old Testament its name. God and the people of Israel entered into a covenant that they would obey Him, and He would have them as His "special treasure above all people". In other words, they would be God's nation.

The basis of this covenant is extremely shaky, since it relies on the obedience of mankind, and this is signified by the mountain quaking:

> *And mount Sinai was altogether on a smoke, because the LORD descended upon it in fire: and the smoke thereof ascended as the smoke of a furnace, and* **the whole mount quaked greatly.** *(Exo 19:18)*

Hebrews 12 shows us the contrast between this Old Covenant and the New Covenant in Jesus Christ, by contrasting the mountains of Sinai and Zion. The difference is that the New Covenant cannot be shaken, as it is built on better promises:

> *For ye are not come unto the mount that might be touched, and that burned with fire, nor unto blackness, and darkness, and tempest, ... Whose voice then **shook the earth**: but now he hath promised, saying, Yet once more I shake not the earth only, but also heaven. And this word, Yet once more, signifieth **the removing of those things that are shaken**, as of things that are made, **that those things which cannot be shaken may remain**. Wherefore we receiving **a kingdom which cannot be moved**, let us have grace, whereby we may serve God acceptably with reverence and godly fear. (Heb 12:18, 26-28)*

Food for thought

Verse 1 - We are now three months into the wilderness journey and we arrive at Sinai. Numbers 33 provides a very useful summary of the wilderness journey, and it is useful to use it as a basis for fitting the events of the wilderness journey as recorded in Exodus and Numbers into a time frame.

Verse 23 - Early in the wilderness journey Moses presumed, or so it seemed, that Israel would obey what God had commanded. Hence he told God that the people would not break through as they had been told not to do so. As time goes on Moses realises that the people are stiff-necked and disobedient and cannot be trusted to obey God's word.

Exodus 20

Draw near, or draw back?

In this chapter we see that Moses drew near to God, whereas the people were too frightened to do so. They stood far off:

> And all the people saw the thunderings, and the lightnings, and the noise of the trumpet, and the mountain smoking: and when the people saw it, **they removed, and stood afar off**. And they said unto Moses, Speak thou with us, and we will hear: but let not God speak with us, lest we die. And Moses said unto the people, Fear not: for God is come to prove you, and that his fear may be before your faces, that ye sin not. And **the people stood afar off, and Moses drew near** unto the thick darkness where God was. (Exo 20:18-21)

We see here two opposites. In Hebrews we're told Moses was afraid, like the people, yet he had the faith to draw near:

> *And so terrible was the sight, that Moses said, I exceedingly fear and quake. (Heb 12:21)*

They were all afraid of the thunder, lightning, smoking and noise of the trumpet, so what was the difference between him and them?

The book of Hebrews picks up and comments on this and tells us that we should draw near by faith, after having been cleansed:

> Let us draw near with a true heart in full assurance of faith, having our hearts sprinkled from an evil conscience, and **our bodies washed with pure water**. (Heb 10:22)

Notice that these were the same criteria given to the children of Israel, who had been told to cleanse themselves and not go near their wives for three days.

> And the LORD said unto Moses, Go unto the people, and sanctify them to day and to morrow, and **let them wash their clothes**, And be ready against the third day: for the third day the LORD will come down in the sight of all the people upon mount Sinai. ... And he said unto the people, Be ready against the third day: come not at your wives. (Exo 19:10-11, 15)

Had they been disobedient and slept with their wives anyway? Had they not cleansed themselves?

The noise, blackness, thunder, were all there to make the people think twice about how to approach God. It required faith to approach God when it was so scary. So for those who had been disobedient and not carried out the command to wash and stay away from their wives, their feelings of guilt would make this fear unbearable.

> And they said unto Moses, Speak thou with us, and we will hear: but let not God speak with us, lest we die. (Exo 20:19)

Hebrews tells us that, for us, the fear has been taken away. There is now a new way to approach God, based on a new mountain. Not Sinai, but Zion:

> *For ye are not come unto the mount that might be touched, and that burned with fire, nor unto blackness, and darkness, and tempest, and the sound of a trumpet, and the voice of words; which voice they that heard intreated that the word should not be spoken to them any more: (for they could not endure that which was commanded, and if so much as a beast touch the mountain, it shall be stoned, or thrust through with a dart: and so terrible was the sight, that Moses said, I exceedingly fear and quake:) but ye are come unto mount Sion ... to Jesus the mediator of the new covenant, and to the blood of sprinkling, that speaketh better things than that of Abel. (Heb 12:18-24)*

Jesus is the mediator of a new covenant. Not this old covenant made at Sinai, in which the people were afraid of the consequences of their sin, and therefore could not approach God. A new covenant where our sins may be forgiven, and, having been fully cleansed from our sins, we may approach our Father in full assurance of faith:

> *Now the just shall live by faith: but if any man draw back, my soul shall have no pleasure in him. But we are not of them who draw back unto perdition; but of them that believe to the saving of the soul. (Heb 10:38-39)*

Food for thought

Verses 8-10 - "remember the sabbath" as one of the commandments, linked with the mention of creation, indicates that Israel were well aware of the Genesis account of creation and we must conclude that the sabbath was already being observed. The Law of Moses now builds it into a codified form of laws.

Verses 24-25 - The injunctions about how Israel were to make altars were to show them that they could not have any input into the way in which God was to be worshipped. He laid out the conditions, Israel had to obey. Likewise the same is true for us. We cannot bring our "wisdom" to our worship. We must follow carefully what He has instructed.

Exodus 21

O how love I thy law!

> *Now these are the judgments which thou shalt set before them.*
> *(Exo 21:1)*

These are the first *"judgements"* given to Israel, after the Ten Commandments. The *judgements* are ways in which to decide in a court of law. They are principles to govern daily life and society as a whole. They ensure fairness and justice is upheld. These were necessary now, because Israel was to be a nation of its own, no longer governed by the laws of Egypt.

We cannot underestimate the impact these judgements had on the nation. The very fact that a nation had God written laws to govern society would automatically mean that their society would excel in comparison with their neighbours. Take for example the fact that they were told not to eat bats, something we only now realise can bring about a global pandemic:

> *And these are they which ye shall have in abomination among the fowls; they shall not be eaten, they are an abomination: the eagle, and the ossifrage, and the ospray ... And the stork, the heron after*

her kind, and the lapwing, and the bat. (Lev 11:13, 19)

Other nations would look at these laws and see how far above their own wisdom Gods judgements in Israelite society were:

> Keep therefore and do them; for this is your wisdom and your understanding in the sight of the nations, which shall hear all these statutes, and say, Surely this great nation is a wise and understanding people. For what nation is there so great, who hath God so nigh unto them, as the LORD our God is in all things that we call upon him for? And what nation is there so great, that hath statutes and judgments so righteous as all this law, which I set before you this day? (Deu 4:5-8)

God's judgements would directly contribute to the stability and prosperity of the nation, which would be like a beacon to the Gentiles. Do we see the law in this light? David said, "Oh, how I love Your law! I think about it all the time!"

> O how love I thy law! it is my meditation all the day. (Psa 119:97)

Food for thought

Verse 6 - That the servant is brought to the "door post" with his ear "bored" may be an indication that the servant would listen to the law, which was to be written "upon the door posts of thine house" (Deut 11:20).

Verse 13 - We are still at Sinai. However God indicates here, in advance, the provision that He will make. That provision was the cities of refuge.

Exodus 22

God protects the fatherless and the widow

Consider the importance of this chapter in terms of the Israelite nation. It is only the second chapter of commandments after they have been made a new nation by God at Sinai. So they are listening carefully to Moses as he expounds God's laws to them for the first time — laws to govern their new nation in their new land of promise.

We read in v22-24 and v25-27 that God will personally protect widows, the fatherless and the poor,

> *Ye shall not afflict any widow, or fatherless child. If thou afflict them in any wise, and they cry at all unto me, I will surely hear their cry; and my wrath shall wax hot, and I will kill you with the sword; and your wives shall be widows, and your children fatherless. (Exo 22:22-24)*

and they should have taken great notice of this. Note the stark warning:

> <u>your</u> *wives shall be widows, and* <u>your</u> *children fatherless.*

The reason for God's hot anger would be because He is gracious to the poor and needy, and His laws are a way of providing for them:

> *If thou lend money to any of my people that is poor by thee, thou shalt not be to him as an usurer, neither shalt thou lay upon him usury. If thou at all take thy neighbour's raiment to pledge, thou shalt deliver it unto him by that the sun goeth down: for that is his covering only, it is his raiment for his skin: wherein shall he sleep? and it shall come to pass, when he crieth unto me, that I will hear;* **for I am gracious.** (Exo 22:25-27)

So when God's righteous laws were cast aside, the widow, poor and fatherless would suffer. That's because much of this law exists to protect this group in particular. As you read on in the Old Testament account of Israel, notice how often God makes good on His promise to punish them when His laws are cast aside, and the poor suffer as a result. Ultimately God's judgement on the nation would be as a result of their disobedience, in their dealing with the poor and needy:

> *Behold, the princes of Israel ... in the midst of thee have they dealt by oppression with the stranger: in thee have they vexed the fatherless and the widow. Thou hast despised mine holy things, and hast profaned my sabbaths ... Behold, therefore I have smitten mine hand at thy dishonest gain which thou hast made, and at thy blood which hath been in the midst of thee ... I will scatter thee among the heathen, and disperse thee in the countries, and will consume thy filthiness out of thee.* (Eze 22:6-8, 13-15)

So God does not punish because He is vindictive, but because He loves the poor, fatherless and widow.

Food for thought

Verse 1 - King David clearly understood the requirements of the law, because when Nathan told him the parable in 2 Samuel 12, David quoted this requirement (see 2 Sam 12:6) as the appropriate restitution that had to be paid for the sin spoken of in the parable.

Verse 25 - This injunction about not lending money out on usury (interest) is seen to be violated in Israel's history, for example in the days when Israel returned from Babylon – Nehemiah 5:7.

Exodus 23

Balance

Have you noticed the balanced teaching in this law? When judging the case of a poor man, it can be tempting to give their word less credibility, and therefore judge a case wrongly based on their lowly status:

> *You shall not pervert the judgment of your poor in his dispute. (Exo 23:6 NKJV)*

But if you are compassionate, it is just as tempting to show favouritism to a poor man in his case:

> *You shall not show partiality to a poor man in his dispute. (Exo 23:3 NKJV)*

The chapter is telling us that both of these are equally wrong.

Taking another example; God looks after the animals, and in the law He allowed for them to be provided for:

> *But the seventh year thou shalt let it rest and lie still; that the poor*

> *of thy people may eat: and what they leave the beasts of the field shall eat. In like manner thou shalt deal with thy vineyard, and with thy oliveyard. (Exo 23:11)*

Yet this does not mean animals should always be allowed to increase. In fact, God counselled the people not to allow wild beasts to become too numerous:

> *And I will send hornets before thee, which shall drive out the Hivite, the Canaanite, and the Hittite, from before thee. I will not drive them out from before thee in one year; lest the land become desolate, and the beast of the field multiply against thee. (Exo 23:28-29)*

Balance has to exist in the law of the land.

For every case where someone is hated, there is someone who hates. Thus if you hate someone, first you need to look to yourself:

> *If thou meet thine enemy's ox or his ass going astray, thou shalt surely bring it back to him again. (Exo 23:4)*

And if you have someone who hates you, and you are tempted to return this hatred, then beware lest you become like him:

> *If thou see the ass of him that hateth thee lying under his burden, and wouldest forbear to help him, thou shalt surely help with him. (Exo 23:5)*

So as we have seen in these examples, there is balance in the law which God gave to Israel. The law recognises that we are fickle and easily won over by sin. We can favour someone wrongly just as easily as dismiss someone whom we should favour. We can go all in for for a cause that seems right, and then be overcome by that cause. We can be hated, and end up being the hater in return. In each of these cases, God shows us a balanced approach.

How do you think we can take the principles laid out in this chapter and apply them to our own lives?

Driving out the inhabitants of the promised land

In this chapter God promises to drive out the inhabitants of the land promised to Abraham, and to establish the children of Israel in it:

> *And I will send hornets before thee, which shall drive out the Hivite, the Canaanite, and the Hittite, from before thee ... And I will set thy bounds from the Red sea even unto the sea of the Philistines, and from the desert unto the river: for I will deliver the inhabitants of the land into your hand; and thou shalt drive them out before thee. (Exo 23:28, 31)*

Their responsibility, stated quite clearly and categorically here, is not to allow those idolatrous and wicked nations to cause them to fall away in their worship of the one true God:

> *Thou shalt make no covenant with them, nor with their gods. They shall not dwell in thy land, lest they make thee sin against me: for if thou serve their gods, it will surely be a snare unto thee. (Exo 23:32-33)*

The warning here is that if any of these people remained, they would be a snare to cause them to sin. This warning came true soon after they inherited the land:

And ye shall make no league with the inhabitants of this land; ye shall throw down their altars: but ye have not obeyed my voice: why have ye done this? ... they shall be as thorns in your sides, and their gods shall be a snare unto you ... And the children of Israel did evil in the sight of the LORD, and served Baalim: and they forsook the LORD God of their fathers, which brought them out of the land of Egypt, and followed other gods, of the gods of the people that were round about them, and bowed themselves unto them, and provoked the LORD to anger. And they forsook the LORD, and served Baal and Ashtaroth. (Jdg 2:2-3, 11-13)

Food for thought

Verse 9 - One might have thought that the period of captivity in Egypt was just a difficult time for Israel. However, God now uses their experience as a means of instructing them how they should treat others. Does our life's experience help us to understand others?

Verses 24-26 - Note that God promised to take sickness away from Israel, but it was conditional on their obedience. So when Jesus came to Israel and found multitudes of sick (e.g. Mark 6:56), it may be that this passage is being alluded to.

Exodus 24

The hidden man

Notice that God asks certain people to come up the mountain, but they are to keep their distance:

> *And he said unto Moses, Come up unto the LORD, thou, and Aaron, Nadab, and Abihu, and seventy of the elders of Israel; and worship ye **afar off**. (Exo 24:1)*

This separation is emphasised a second time so that the point is driven home. They are not to come near:

> *And Moses alone shall come near the LORD: but **they shall not come nigh**; neither shall the people go up with him. (Exo 24:2)*

Moses, only, was to come near to God, and everyone else had to stay away. It's curious, isn't it?

Remember that at the first occasion at the mountain, God had told all the people to stay back. He had created fire and smoke to scare them so that they would obey:

> And all the people saw the thunderings, and the lightnings, and the noise of the trumpet, and the mountain smoking: and when the people saw it, they removed, and stood afar off. And they said unto Moses, Speak thou with us, and we will hear: but let not God speak with us, lest we die. And Moses said unto the people, Fear not: for God is come to prove you, and that his fear may be before your faces, that ye sin not. (Exo 20:18-20)

So Moses was special. He was able to draw near to God, whilst everyone else had to stay back. But wait a minute - there's someone else not mentioned here. Someone else —mentioned almost in passing — came with Moses to meet God:

> And Moses rose up, and his minister Joshua: and Moses went up into the mount of God. (Exo 24:13)

It seems that Moses took Joshua with him. Moses was in the mountain for forty days, and Joshua appears to have been with him the whole time.

The lesson for us is to look behind the words presented to us in the word of God. We need to search for these hidden gems that are hidden in plain sight. The point here is that Joshua, while not being anyone of standing, neither a priest nor leader of the people, was the one who got to draw near to the presence of God. By being a servant he gained the greatest privilege.

> But he that is greatest among you shall be your servant. And whosoever shall exalt himself shall be abased; and he that shall humble himself shall be exalted. (Mat 23:11-12)

The writer in the Proverbs recognised this and told a parable. A spider may be small, but, unlike those who try to gain entry to the king by their own merit, she dwells in the palace all the time:

The spider taketh hold with her hands, and is in kings' palaces. (Pro 30:28)

Food for thought

Verse 1 - Notice that Eleazar and Ithamar - the other two sons of Aaron - are not mentioned here and did not ascend the mount with Moses and Aaron. Possibly being singled out like this caused Nadab and Abihu to think a bit more highly of themselves than they should have — hence they took liberties and offered "strange fire" Lev 10:1.

Verse 14 - Moses' charge to the elders is seen in the way Jesus spoke to his disciples during the last night of his life on earth – Matt 26:36,38,40. Moses went into the mountain to communicate with God. Jesus, likewise, communicated with his Father.

Exodus 25

A burden too heavy to carry

Have you noticed that the mercy seat, on top of the ark, is the same size as the ark itself? Can you imagine how heavy this would be to carry?

> *And they shall make an ark of shittim wood: two cubits and a half shall be the length thereof, and a cubit and a half the breadth thereof, and a cubit and a half the height thereof ... And thou shalt make a mercy seat of pure gold: two cubits and a half shall be the length thereof, and a cubit and a half the breadth thereof. (Exo 25:10, 17)*

A cubit is about half a yard (45cm) long, so the ark and mercy seat could have been about 1 1/2 yards (113 cm) long and 3/4 yard (68 cm) wide... and the mercy seat was solid gold!

As well as the seat, cherubim, and ark of gold (or covered in gold), the ark bore the stone tablets which were also heavy. How on earth could the Levites carry it?

> *And thou shalt cast four rings of gold for it, and put them in the*

*four corners thereof; and two rings shall be in the one side of it, and two rings in the other side of it. And thou shalt make staves of shittim wood, and overlay them with gold. And thou shalt put the staves into the rings by the sides of the ark, **that the ark may be borne with them**.* (Exo 25:12-14)

There is an interesting occurrence at the time of David, where David was trying to bring the ark to him in Jerusalem. Presumably due to its great weight, he decided to put it on a cart:

And they carried the ark of God in a new cart out of the house of Abinadab: and Uzza and Ahio drave the cart ... And when they came unto the threshingfloor of Chidon, Uzza put forth his hand to hold the ark; for the oxen stumbled. And the anger of the LORD was kindled against Uzza, and he smote him, because he put his hand to the ark: and there he died before God. (1Ch 13:7, 9-10)

Clearly this was not the way to go about it, as David himself realised:

Then David said, None ought to carry the ark of God but the Levites: for them hath the LORD chosen to carry the ark of God, and to minister unto him for ever. (1Ch 15:2)

The result was that David had to have faith that what God had said should be done (carrying the ark) was possible, even though it didn't seem to be.

In faith the Levites took their places under the staves and lifted up the ark, then carried it up the difficult incline to the city of David. And the record states that God helped them:

So David, and the elders of Israel, and the captains over thousands,

> went to bring up the ark of the covenant of the LORD out of the house of Obededom with joy. And it came to pass, when **God helped the Levites that bare the ark** of the covenant of the LORD, that they offered seven bullocks and seven rams. (1Ch 15:25-26)

The lesson here is that what God asks us to do may be difficult at times, but if we are obedient and have faith, He will help.

> Let us therefore come boldly unto the throne of grace, that we may obtain mercy, and find grace to help in time of need. (Heb 4:16)
> But without faith it is impossible to please him: for he that cometh to God must believe that he is, and that he is a rewarder of them that diligently seek him. (Heb 11:6)

Food for thought

Verse 2 - Notice that Moses was to accept that which was given "willingly". God was not interested in gifts that were given grudgingly. The same is true of ourselves. In fact Paul, quoting what Jesus had said, teaches that the Lord loves a cheerful giver - 2 Cor 9:7

Verse 8 - "That I may dwell among them" shows God's desire to fellowship mankind. The way that this phrase – a rare phrase in Scripture – is picked up in Psalm 68:18 shows how that dwelling is to be achieved. It is not through the tabernacle in the wilderness. It is to be through the death and resurrection of Jesus, which is what Psalm 68 is talking about – see Ephesians 4:8.

Exodus 26

The structural detail of the Tabernacle

Have you noticed that this structure is perfectly designed for a travelling people? The modern analogy we might use, and I don't mean to be flippant, is of a travelling circus tent. This is large, semi permanent (it stays in place for weeks at a time) but has to be erected and taken down quickly and transported from place to place. Thus it needs to be lightweight, pack up into a small space, easy to assemble, break up into small parts that can be carried by hand, and flexible enough to be built without a foundation.

The difference in law between a permanent and non-permanent building is based on whether it has a foundation or not. A foundation is something only permanent buildings have. It creates a flat base upon which to build so that the building remains square and level. It is hard and heavy so that the building doesn't subside. A foundation is wider than the walls of a building so that it spreads the weight over the maximum surface area. But a foundation, as desirable as it is, is unwieldy and non-transportable. It takes a long time to make, and it can't be removed once it's in place. In 1 Kings 7:10 we are told this detail about the foundation of the temple in Jerusalem — the foundation stones were big and costly:

> And the foundation was of costly stones, even great stones, stones of ten cubits, and stones of eight cubits. (1Ki 7:10)

You can still see these today in Jerusalem adjacent to the Western (Wailing) Wall. Having lasted thousands of years we could say they're as permanent as permanent can be!

So the tabernacle was non permanent, as it didn't have a foundation, but was it actually a tent? Notice in verse 15 that it was made of boards:

> And thou shalt make boards for the tabernacle of shittim wood standing up. (Exo 26:15)

This is the same kind of construction used in some houses today. Rigid timber boards (actually, panels made up of boards, with a frame and insulation) are stood upon a foundation and then screwed together to form the wall of the house. It's a much faster and more accurate way to build houses, only recently discovered in modern times, yet here in the Bible we have a design for such a building thousands of years earlier. The really amazing thing about the design of the Tabernacle, though, is that the boards had no foundations to go onto, and yet worked fine.

The staggeringly simple detail that made the whole building work without a foundation was the "sockets" spoken of in verse 19:

> And thou shalt make forty sockets of silver under the twenty boards; two sockets under one board for his two tenons, and two sockets under another board for his two tenons. (Exo 26:19)

These could be hammered or fixed into the ground. Once this was done, a board could be carried to the sockets and placed with the bottom of the board on two sockets - while still lying on the ground. I think the sockets looked more or less like the birthday candle holder you saw on your last birthday cake! Imagine two pins in the bottom of the board, inserted into a hole in each socket. With the bottom of the board unable to move, it would be simple to lift the other end of the board, with perhaps two people, and push the board upright. Once upright it could be tethered with ropes and tent pegs. This construction is truly amazing when you consider that it takes into account any undulating or non-level ground that the children of Israel would have encountered. Once the boards were all in place, there would be a wall almost as solid as any permanent building. This was no ordinary tent.

Apart from the practical reasons for the tabernacle being made in this way, there was a further spiritual significance. In Corinthians we read:

> *For other foundation can no man lay than that is laid, which is Jesus Christ. (1Co 3:11)*

The tabernacle, which was constructed before Jesus, signified that the revelation from God about salvation was incomplete. The most important part, Jesus himself, hadn't been revealed yet. It is indicative of the life led by faith, which sees only incomplete detail of salvation, yet has faith that the rest will be taken care of by God.

> *By faith [Abraham] dwelt in the land of promise as in a foreign country, dwelling in tents with Isaac and Jacob, the heirs with him of the same promise; for he waited for the city which has foundations, whose builder and maker is God. (Heb 11:9-10 NKJV)*

Food for thought

Verse 24 - In saying that the boards were to be "coupled" together we are introduced to an idea which is applied to Jerusalem (Psalm 122:3) where the same word is translated as "compacted". The tabernacle was a foreshadowing of something more permanent - the "city which has foundations" (see Heb 11:10). That is not Jerusalem which is now, but the heavenly Jerusalem (see Heb 12:22).

Verse 30 - The repetition of the command that the tabernacle should be built according to the pattern shown, really makes it clear that God requires that things of His making be made as He requires. The body of Christ (the believers) is His building. We must, therefore, realise that the way in which we "build" it must be according to the pattern laid out in Scripture. Man-made rules are not acceptable.

Exodus 27

Those who had prepared oil

Keeping the lamp burning continually was the personal responsibility of Aaron, the High Priest. This was obviously too important to delegate. But presumably because this was a round-the-clock task, he was allowed to use his own sons to do it, but no-one else. However, the oil for the lamps was brought by the people themselves, presumably whoever saw it as their duty, and had the means to do so:

> And thou shalt command the children of Israel, that they bring thee pure oil olive beaten for the light, to cause the lamp to burn always. In the tabernacle of the congregation without the vail, which is before the testimony, Aaron and his sons shall order it from evening to morning before the LORD: it shall be a statute for ever unto their generations on the behalf of the children of Israel. (Exo 27:20-21)

Producing oil is no small task, nor is it a quick one. Firstly the olive tree has to be grown, then the olives harvested, then pressed, then the oil beaten, then stored, then transported, and finally stored again and used by the priest in the lamp.

Jesus seems to be making this point when he speaks of the parable of the ten virgins. Five had prepared, and the other five had not:

> *Then shall the kingdom of heaven be likened unto ten virgins, which took their lamps, and went forth to meet the bridegroom. And five of them were wise, and five were foolish. They that were foolish took their lamps, and took no oil with them: but the wise took oil in their vessels with their lamps. (Mat 25:1-4)*

Yet for each of these, there came the day when their own lamps needed oil, and only the ones who had been personally prepared, had that oil available:

> *Then all those virgins arose, and trimmed their lamps. And the foolish said unto the wise, Give us of your oil; for our lamps are gone out. But the wise answered, saying, Not so; lest there be not enough for us and you: but go ye rather to them that sell, and buy for yourselves. (Mat 25:7-9)*

The point is that for us, the time will come when it is our own supply of oil, not that of others, that will matter. The collection of oil for the Israelites was a national one, and so it would have been relatively easy to be carried along by the preparation of others more diligent than themselves. Likewise we may well be able to get through most of our lives relying on the spiritual example or nourishment of others, but one day Jesus will return and will check whether he knows us personally:

> *And while they went to buy, the bridegroom came; and they that were ready went in with him to the marriage: and the door was shut. Afterward came also the other virgins, saying, Lord, Lord,*

open to us. But he answered and said, Verily I say unto you, I know you not. (Mat 25:10-12)

Food for thought

Verses 3-7 - The fact that staves are described along with their purpose – to carry the altar – is an indication that the tabernacle was to be seen as a mobile structure. Israel were on a journey and their God was going to travel with them, as he assured David that He did (2 Sam 7:6-7).

Verse 20 - Whereas Israel had to give willingly for the manufacture of the tabernacle (Exo 25:2) they were "commanded" to bring pure olive oil. Whereas the structure of the tabernacle represented the congregation and required the willingness of the members to make it work, the oil for the lamps represented the word of God, and as such was not left to the discretion of man. Likewise whatever we do in "building the house of God", we must give attention to Scripture to guide us.

Exodus 28

Wisdom is more precious than rubies

The variety of precious gemstones that went into the breastplate (twelve in all) shows us that mineral mining had been part of society for quite some time:

> And thou shalt set in it settings of stones, even four rows of stones: the first row shall be a sardius, a topaz, and a carbuncle: this shall be the first row. And the second row shall be an emerald, a sapphire, and a diamond. And the third row a ligure, an agate, and an amethyst. And the fourth row a beryl, and an onyx, and a jasper: they shall be set in gold in their inclosings. (Exo 28:17-20)

How do you think the children of Israel, formerly a slave people, got such gems? The topaz, for example, is said in the book of Job to come from Ethiopia, a neighbour to Egypt:

> The topaz of Ethiopia shall not equal it, neither shall it be valued with pure gold. (Job 28:19)

It seems that God, in His foreknowledge, had provided for this occasion.

When the children of Israel left Egypt, He had commanded them to "plunder" the Egyptians, and the record tells us that this included jewellery:

> *And the children of Israel did according to the word of Moses; and they borrowed of the Egyptians jewels of silver, and jewels of gold, and raiment: and the LORD gave the people favour in the sight of the Egyptians, so that they lent unto them such things as they required. And they spoiled the Egyptians.* (Exo 12:35-36)

At the time of Solomon we are told of the precious stones the Queen of Sheba brought Solomon, also presumably from Ethiopia or near there:

> *And she came to Jerusalem with a very great train, with camels that bare spices, and very much gold, and precious stones: and when she was come to Solomon, she communed with him of all that was in her heart.* (1Ki 10:2)

The point being made here is that the precious stones were traded to obtain wisdom, and therefore wisdom is more precious even than those precious stones. Wisdom is what was embodied in the design of the breastplate, which we are told was the "breastplate of judgment" of the priest. Wisdom is what we should seek after, as the Queen of Sheba did:

> *Happy is the man that findeth wisdom, and the man that getteth understanding. For the merchandise of it is better than the merchandise of silver, and the gain thereof than fine gold. She is more precious than rubies: and all the things thou canst desire are not to be compared unto her.* (Pro 3:13-15)

Food for thought

Verse 1 - In taking Aaron from "from among the children of Israel" we are being shown that the high priest must share the nature and experiences of those he serves (see also the next chapter). This is true to Jesus also (Hebrews 5:1).

Verses 42-43 - When the priests offered sacrifices before God they were clothed in special garments. The breeches spoken of here would be covered by the outer garments. However, the requirement was that they were worn even though they were not seen. In like manner our covering in Christ is not visible.

Exodus 29

A priest "made like unto his brethren".

And I will sanctify the tabernacle of the congregation, and the altar: I will sanctify also both Aaron and his sons, to minister to me in the priest's office. (Exo 29:44)

This chapter records what was to be done on the seven days of cleansing for Aaron and his sons prior to their consecration as priests:

And thus shalt thou do unto Aaron, and to his sons, according to all things which I have commanded thee: seven days shalt thou consecrate them ... Seven days thou shalt make an atonement for the altar, and sanctify it; and it shall be an altar most holy: whatsoever toucheth the altar shall be holy. (Exo 29:35, 37)

One of the reasons the books of the law seem so long is that there is repetition. First it records God telling Moses how to carry out His wishes, then later the actual event is recorded. In this particular chapter, we need to remember that Moses is still on Sinai receiving Gods instructions:

And Moses went up into the mount, and a cloud covered the mount. And the glory of the LORD abode upon mount Sinai, and the cloud covered it six days: and the seventh day he called unto Moses out of the midst of the cloud ... And Moses went into the midst of the cloud, and gat him up into the mount: and Moses was in the mount forty days and forty nights. And the LORD spake unto Moses, saying, ... (Exo 24:15-18, 25:1)

We're now in chapter 29, but nothing further has happened. The consecration of Aaron wasn't happening at this point either — it would come to pass in Leviticus 8 & 9. This tells us something extremely interesting. It means that the golden calf incident, which happens in chapter 32, hadn't happened yet. In fact, it was during these forty days, when God was telling Moses about anointing Aaron as priest, that Aaron was making the people a false god, the golden calf:

And when the people saw that Moses delayed to come down out of the mount, the people gathered themselves together unto Aaron, and said unto him, Up, make us gods, which shall go before us; for as for this Moses, the man that brought us up out of the land of Egypt, we wot not what is become of him. And Aaron said unto them, Break off the golden earrings, which are in the ears of your wives, of your sons, and of your daughters, and bring them unto me ... And he received them at their hand, and fashioned it with a graving tool, after he had made it a molten calf: and they said, These be thy gods, O Israel, which brought thee up out of the land of Egypt ... And the LORD said unto Moses, Go, get thee down; for thy people, which thou broughtest out of the land of Egypt, have corrupted themselves... (Exo 32:1-7)

By cleansing Aaron, God was willing to take this man, who had done this thing. He was willing to take a man who had been weak and easily led, and consecrate him to undertake the most important task in the national worship. Why is this?

The reason is that this is a pattern. God is telling us that the real high priest, Jesus, had to have human nature and be tempted in order to be a suitable intercessor for us. Notice how the point is made that Aaron is from "among the people":

> *And take thou unto thee Aaron thy brother, and his sons with him,* ***from among the children of Israel****, that he may minister unto me in the priest's office, even Aaron, Nadab and Abihu, Eleazar and Ithamar, Aaron's sons. (Exo 28:1)*

Which is entirely the reason why Jesus can help us in our times of temptation, and to make intercession for our sins:

> *Wherefore in all things it behoved him* ***to be made like unto his brethren****, that he might be a merciful and faithful high priest in things pertaining to God, to make reconciliation for the sins of the people. For in that he himself hath suffered being tempted, he is able to succour them that are tempted. (Heb 2:17-18)*

Food for thought

Verse 7 - Moses anointed Aaron – but was not anointed himself! Moses was called of God, Aaron's office was by descent. Moses was the basis for "that prophet" – Messiah (e.g John 6:14).

Verse 45 - That God would "dwell among" Israel is a foretaste of His involvement in the body of believers – see 2 Corinthians 6:16-17.

Exodus 30

The perfect incense

The incense altar had to be sprinkled with blood, once a year, on the day of atonement:

> *And Aaron shall make an atonement upon the horns of it once in a year with the blood of the sin offering of atonements: once in the year shall he make atonement upon it throughout your generations: it is most holy unto the LORD. (Exo 30:10)*

This is spoken of in Leviticus 16:

> *And he shall go out unto the altar that is before the LORD, and make an atonement for it; and shall take of the blood of the bullock, and of the blood of the goat, and put it upon the horns of the altar round about. And he shall sprinkle of the blood upon it with his finger seven times, and cleanse it, and hallow it from the uncleanness of the children of Israel. (Lev 16:18-19)*

The timing of the law is very interesting, because Aaron's sons had only just died by offering "strange fire" before the LORD:

> *And the LORD spake unto Moses after the death of the two sons of Aaron, when they offered before the LORD, and died; (Lev 16:1)*

What they had done seems to relate to this same incense altar. Notice where they are when the incident happens:

> *And Nadab and Abihu, the sons of Aaron, took either of them his censer, and put fire therein, and put incense thereon, and offered strange fire **before the LORD**, which he commanded them not. And there went out fire from the LORD, and devoured them, and they died **before the LORD**. (Lev 10:1-2)*

The phrase "before the LORD" is repeated twice, so it seems they were at the veil of the most holy place, where the incense altar was:

> *And thou shalt put it before the vail that is by the ark of the testimony, before the mercy seat that is over the testimony, where I will meet with thee. ... And when Aaron lighteth the lamps at even, he shall burn incense upon it, a perpetual incense **before the LORD** throughout your generations. (Exo 30:6, 8)*

So we can make a very educated guess that what the two sons of Aaron were doing, was using the wrong incense upon this altar, rather than the specific incense that the LORD God commanded them to use. The warning is written right here in Exodus 30, in the same place as the design for the incense altar:

> ***Ye shall offer no strange incense thereon**, nor burnt sacrifice, nor meat offering; neither shall ye pour drink offering thereon. (Exo 30:9)*

Notice the similarity in wording ("strange") that confirms that this is, in all probability, what Nadab and Abihu did:

> *And Nadab and Abihu, the sons of Aaron, took either of them his censer, and put fire therein, and **put incense thereon, and offered strange fire** before the LORD, which he commanded them not. (Lev 10:1)*

It is a very worrying incident for you and me because we might think that there is no way for us to approach God that is Holy enough, or correct enough, in our own prayers or worship.

And yet, digging a little deeper, we see that the recipe for the incense was already provided. The sons of Aaron simply needed to stick to it, and not change anything. It's provided in this very same chapter:

> *And the LORD said unto Moses, Take unto thee sweet spices, stacte, and onycha, and galbanum; these sweet spices with pure frankincense: of each shall there be a like weight: and thou shalt make it a perfume, a confection after the art of the apothecary, tempered together, pure and holy: and thou shalt beat some of it very small, and put of it before the testimony in the tabernacle of the congregation, where I will meet with thee: it shall be unto you most holy. (Exo 30:34-36)*

Notice the phrase "it shall be unto you most holy." This incense, or "perfume", was special and unique. Not only did that same recipe have to be used every time without fail, but it was also prohibited to use it for anything else:

> *And as for the perfume which thou shalt make, ye shall not make to yourselves according to the composition thereof: it shall be unto*

thee holy for the LORD. Whosoever shall make like unto that, to smell thereto, shall even be cut off from his people. (Exo 30:37-38)

In Revelation, it is revealed to us that this incense speaks of our prayers to God:

And another angel came and stood at the altar, having a golden censer; and there was given unto him much incense, that he should offer it with the prayers of all saints upon the golden altar which was before the throne. And the smoke of the incense, which came with the prayers of the saints, ascended up before God out of the angel's hand. (Rev 8:3-4)

It shows us that we have to be respectful when we approach God in prayer. Jesus gave us the recipe when his disciples asked him how they should pray. We should notice here that Jesus is not at all vague in his answer. He gives a specific pattern, and like that recipe for the incense, it is unambiguous:

And he said unto them, When ye pray, say, Our Father which art in heaven, Hallowed be thy name. Thy kingdom come. Thy will be done, as in heaven, so in earth. Give us day by day our daily bread. And forgive us our sins; for we also forgive every one that is indebted to us. And lead us not into temptation; but deliver us from evil. (Luk 11:2-4)

So should we only ever use this pattern without embellishment or variation?

Hebrews 9 speaks at length about the pattern of the tabernacle (including this incense altar), and how it applies to Jesus Christ. This original tabernacle was merely a pattern of better things to come:

> *Now when these things were thus ordained, the priests went always into the first tabernacle, accomplishing the service of God. But into the second went the high priest alone once every year, not without blood, which he offered for himself, and for the errors of the people ... Which was a figure for the time then present, in which were offered both gifts and sacrifices, that could not make him that did the service perfect, as pertaining to the conscience;* (Heb 9:6-7, 9)

Jesus is the fulfilment of that pattern, able to take our inadequate prayers and mediate on our behalf to God, without danger to us:

> *But Christ being come an high priest of good things to come, by a greater and more perfect tabernacle, not made with hands, that is to say, not of this building; Neither by the blood of goats and calves, but by his own blood he entered in once into the holy place, having obtained eternal redemption for us. For if the blood of bulls and of goats, and the ashes of an heifer sprinkling the unclean, sanctifieth to the purifying of the flesh: how much more shall the blood of Christ, who through the eternal Spirit offered himself without spot to God, purge your conscience from dead works to serve the living God?* (Heb 9:11-14)

The work of the Lord Jesus Christ allows us to approach God with a clear conscience despite our inadequacies and failings, and the imperfect form of our prayers:

> *Having therefore, brethren, boldness to enter into the holiest by the blood of Jesus, by a new and living way, which he hath consecrated for us, through the veil, that is to say, his flesh; and having an high priest over the house of God; let us draw near with a true heart in full assurance of faith, having our hearts sprinkled from*

an evil conscience, and our bodies washed with pure water. (Heb 10:19-22)

Food for thought

Verse 13 - This "half shekel" payment could be the basis for Matthew 17:27, where, in response to the question as to whether Jesus paid taxes, Peter found a coin in the fish's mouth. The coin was "for me and thee" Jesus said, which makes it half a coin each.

Verses 18-19 - The laver for washing is typical of the Word of God - the Word washes us - Ephesians 5:26.

Exodus 31

The master craftsman

We meet someone in this chapter who is unique and very special, but his name is not well known like Moses or Aaron:

See, I have called by name Bezaleel the son of Uri, the son of Hur, of the tribe of Judah. (Exo 31:2)

God had given him wisdom in all kinds of building and engraving work:

And I have filled him with the spirit of God, in wisdom, and in understanding, and in knowledge, and in all manner of workmanship, to devise cunning works, to work in gold, and in silver, and in brass, and in cutting of stones, to set them, and in carving of timber, to work in all manner of workmanship. (Exo 31:3-5)

This must have been an extremely impressive individual, and he was the one God ordained to lead the work of the building of the tabernacle. We see, then, that when God wants something doing, He not only provides the materials and plans, but also the right people to do it. When the Bible says "I have filled him with **the spirit of God…**" it means that a mind-set similar to God's creative mind was in him:

> And the earth was without form, and void; and darkness was upon the face of the deep. And **the Spirit of God** moved upon the face of the waters. (Gen 1:2)

This creative wisdom, the spirit of God, is described as a "master craftsman" in Proverbs, when speaking of the creation:

> Then I was beside Him as a master craftsman; and I was daily His delight, rejoicing always before Him. (Pro 8:30 NKJV)

As an engineer by trade, I find it awe-inspiring to think that God could influence a man to obtain some of the same expertise and skill that God Himself had in creating the world. We're accustomed to thinking of the New Testament apostles who obtained gifts of language and healing, but not so much to thinking of building work and artistic talent. What we're being told here is that this person, Bezaleel, was capable of bringing to fruition building structures and engraved work, the likes of which had never been seen before.

But the record doesn't stop with Bezaleel:

> And I, behold, I have given with him Aholiab, the son of Ahisamach, of the tribe of Dan: and **in the hearts of all that are wise hearted I have put wisdom**, that they may make all that I have commanded thee. (Exo 31:6)

We see that, in fact, there was a whole group of people whom God gave wisdom to do this wonderful work of the creating of His tabernacle, ark, mercy seat, furniture and equipment.

These people were a foreshadowing of how God would work in Jesus and the Apostles to establish the gospel and to bring it to the Gentiles. This same creative wisdom (the spirit of God) was at work in Jesus, the master craftsman, and the apostles, in setting up the "household of God", ready for God to inhabit as His dwelling:

> *Now therefore ye are no more strangers and foreigners, but fellowcitizens with the saints, and of the household of God; and are built upon the foundation of the apostles and prophets, Jesus Christ himself being the chief corner stone; in whom all the building fitly framed together groweth unto an holy temple in the Lord: in whom ye also are builded together for an habitation of God through the Spirit. (Eph 2:19-22)*

Food for thought

Verse 2 - Either Hur was a very old man when he held up Moses' arms (Exodus 17:12) or Bezaleel was a very young man, because he was the grandson of Hur, and yet we are still only two years into the wilderness journey.

Verse 13 - The Sabbath provided Israel with relief from the toil of the ground which was given to Adam (Gen 3:17-19), as a foretaste of the kingdom.

Exodus 32

Joshua, the servant

In this chapter we have another indication of how close to Moses Joshua was:

> And when Joshua heard the noise of the people as they shouted, he said unto Moses, There is a noise of war in the camp. (Exo 32:17)

This passage reveals that Joshua had been on the mountain with Moses for the forty days he was there in the presence of God. He had gone up there as Moses's minister, or servant:

> And the LORD said unto Moses, Come up to me into the mount, and be there: and I will give thee tables of stone, and a law, and commandments which I have written; that thou mayest teach them. And Moses rose up, and his minister Joshua: and Moses went up into the mount of God. (Exo 24:12-13)

We can learn a lot from Joshua's example, who stayed in the background until he was appointed to office. Elisha, Samuel, the apostles, even Jesus, rose to prominence only after first learning in the background. Joshua's humility is demonstrated by having accepted the role as Moses's helper, even after he had led Israel to battle against the Amalekites:

> *And Moses said unto Joshua, Choose us out men, and go out, fight with Amalek: to morrow I will stand on the top of the hill with the rod of God in mine hand. So Joshua did as Moses had said to him, and fought with Amalek: and Moses, Aaron, and Hur went up to the top of the hill. (Exo 17:9-10)*

However, the real point is not that Joshua was humble, but that he was wise. None of the others, being a leader, managed to go up the mountain to receive the law. None of the other leaders were asked to fight the LORD's battles. None of the others had such regular access to Moses, the man of God. The point is that, when there is a great man or woman, it is their servant who gets the most benefit of their wisdom and by seeing them in action in their daily lives. It is their servant who is most likely to be like their master in the end.

The name "Joshua" is the Hebrew version of "Jesus", meaning "The LORD is salvation", and Jesus was ultimately the one who became like Moses in the fullest sense:

> *And he shall send Jesus Christ, which before was preached unto you ... For Moses truly said unto the fathers, A prophet shall the Lord your God raise up unto you of your brethren, like unto me; him shall ye hear in all things whatsoever he shall say unto you. (Act 3:20-22)*

Jesus was able, through study and meditation on the Word of God, to follow the path of Moses and become like him. In turn, we can take the same example, by studying Moses, Joshua, and Jesus, ultimately to become a little like them in the way we live our lives:

> *If I then, your Lord and Master, have washed your feet; ye also ought to wash one another's feet.* For **I have given you an example**, *that ye should do as I have done to you. Verily, verily, I say unto you,* **The servant is not greater than his lord;** *neither he that is sent greater than he that sent him. If ye know these things, happy are ye if ye do them.* (Jhn 13:14-17)

Food for thought

Verse 6 - In sitting down to eat and drink and then rising up to play, the people are very much like Esau (Genesis 25:34), who sold his birthright.

Verse 34 - The promise that "mine angel shall go before thee" is because God was no longer going to be present there with the people. Whilst we might think it was good that God sent an angel, we must understand that the angel was sent because Israel had rebelled in making the golden calf.

Exodus 33

Meeting with God outside the camp

When Israel came out of Egypt and arrived at Sinai, God spoke of making them a holy nation of priests:

> *Ye have seen what I did unto the Egyptians, and how I bare you on eagles' wings, and brought you unto myself. Now therefore, if ye will obey my voice indeed, and keep my covenant, then ye shall be a peculiar treasure unto me above all people: for all the earth is mine: and ye shall be unto me a kingdom of priests, and an holy nation. These are the words which thou shalt speak unto the children of Israel.* (Exo 19:4-6)

Then when Moses was on the mountain receiving instructions as to how this was going to happen, namely the tabernacle and priesthood, and the law, the people made an idol of gold and started worshipping it.

If we check carefully the wording of the passage quoted above, we see that the promise was dependent on their obedience:

> *...if ye will obey my voice indeed, and keep my covenant...*

It is sad, but the children of Israel fell at the first hurdle. By rights they should not now be a special people, or a holy nation, or a kingdom of priests.

What we see next is a withdrawal of these priviledges and a rethinking of the plan God had made. We see that, rather than the tabernacle being built, even Moses takes his tent outside the camp, so that when he meets God it is not within the camp of the people:

> *Moses took his tent and pitched it outside the camp, far from the camp, and called it the tabernacle of meeting. And it came to pass that everyone who sought the LORD went out to the tabernacle of meeting which was outside the camp.* (Exo 33:7 NKJV)

And then God drops this bombshell, saying that instead of being in their midst Himself, He will only send an angel before them:

> *And the LORD said unto Moses, Depart, and go up hence, thou and the people which thou hast brought up out of the land of Egypt, unto the land which I sware unto Abraham, to Isaac, and to Jacob, saying, Unto thy seed will I give it: And I will send an angel before thee ... for I will not go up in the midst of thee; for thou art a stiffnecked people: lest I consume thee in the way.* (Exo 33:1-3)

I think what this means in practice is that God would honour the promises to Abraham, Isaac and Jacob, to give their seed the land, but that this generation would not be His "special treasure". It means that the tabernacle would not be built, despite God having given the plans for it to Moses. It means that there would be no priesthood through Aaron, but that people would have to go outside the camp to Moses in order to commune with God[2].

Such is the consequence of the golden calf incident.

And how about for us? We too sin and fall short. We fall often at the first hurdle. For us there never even has been a promise of being a special nation, replete with God's laws, and a tabernacle of meeting. But for gentiles like us, there is a better promise, because for us there is Jesus, whom we can meet (as it were) outside the camp in prayer, confessing our sins, and who has continual access to the Father on our behalf. Let us realise the privilege we have, to have promises based on God's oath rather than being a covenant based on our obedience:

> *We have an altar, whereof they have no right to eat which serve the tabernacle ... Wherefore Jesus also, that he might sanctify the people with his own blood, suffered without the gate. Let us go forth therefore unto him without the camp, bearing his reproach. (Heb 13:10, 12-13)*

This pattern is there in our chapter, though we may easily have missed it. Joshua, whose name means "Jesus", is there in the presence of God continually:

> *And the LORD spake unto Moses face to face, as a man speaketh unto his friend. And he turned again into the camp: but his servant Joshua, the son of Nun, a young man, departed not out of the tabernacle. (Exo 33:11)*

---

[2] But see what happens in the next two chapters.

Food for thought

Verse 1 - In God's reference to the "land which I sware unto Abraham, to Isaac and Jacob" we are being introduced to a phrase that Joseph used (Genesis 50:24) when encouraging the children in Israel to take his bones with them when they left Egypt. In fact the phrase is only used originally that one time, and then many times in connection with Moses (Exodus 33:1, Numbers 32:11, Deuteronomy 1:8, 6:10, 9:5, 30:20, 34:4). It is a refrain that Israel were to take hold of to remind them of the faith of Joseph.

Verses 15-16 - Moses' concern, after the incident of the golden calf, was that he was going to be left on his own to take Israel to the land of promise, and that if the tabernacle wasn't built, the nations around would not know that God was with them. Hence his questioning God, and the assurance God gave him.

Exodus 34

Forty days without food

Remember that Moses had been up on the mountain with Joshua his servant, and had received ten commandments on two tables of stone. These Moses had broken when he came down the mountain and saw the idolatry that the people were up to in his absence. He now goes up again, and this time, Joshua stays below, and Moses goes up alone:

> *And the LORD said unto Moses, Hew thee two tables of stone like unto the first: and I will write upon these tables the words that were in the first tables, which thou brakest. And be ready in the morning, and come up in the morning unto mount Sinai, and present thyself there to me in the top of the mount. And no man shall come up with thee, neither let any man be seen throughout all the mount; neither let the flocks nor herds feed before that mount.* (Exo 34:1-3)

The immediate practical consequence of going up alone is that Joshua is no longer there to provide food for him, and therefore he goes without food and drink for the duration ... forty days!

> *And he was there with the LORD forty days and forty nights; he did neither eat bread, nor drink water. And he wrote upon the tables the words of the covenant, the ten commandments.* (Exo 34:28)

It is not possible for a man to survive much longer than three days without water, so we know that God sustained him in some miraculous way. We see an echo of this event with Elijah; when he took a trip to this same mountain, he was sustained for forty days without food:

> *And he arose, and did eat and drink, and went in the strength of that meat forty days and forty nights unto Horeb the mount of God.* (1Ki 19:8)

So we have two men, both of whom went to Horeb, and were both sustained miraculously for forty days without bread or water.

On the mountain, alone, Moses is allowed to see the LORD God pass by him and declare to him His glory:

> *And the LORD descended in the cloud, and stood with him there, and proclaimed the name of the LORD. And the LORD passed by before him, and proclaimed, The LORD, The LORD God, merciful and gracious, longsuffering, and abundant in goodness and truth, keeping mercy for thousands, forgiving iniquity and transgression and sin, and that will by no means clear the guilty; visiting the iniquity of the fathers upon the children, and upon the children's children, unto the third and to the fourth generation.* (Exo 34:5-7)

Elijah similarly stood on that mountain while the LORD God passed by:

> *And he said, Go forth, and stand upon the mount before the LORD. And, behold, the LORD passed by, and a great and strong wind rent the mountains, and brake in pieces the rocks before the LORD; but the LORD was not in the wind: and after the wind an earthquake; but the LORD was not in the earthquake...* (1Ki 19:11)

And so we come to a third person who also went without food for forty days. The Lord Jesus:

> *And when he had fasted forty days and forty nights, he was afterward an hungred.* (Mat 4:2)

And, like Moses and Elijah, who entered the presence of God, so Jesus entered the presence of God permanently, in order to make intercession for the sinful men and women who put their trust in him:

> *For Christ is not entered into the holy places made with hands, which are the figures of the true; but into heaven itself, now to appear in the presence of God for us.* (Heb 9:24)

Food for thought

Verse 6 - The way in which God showed His character to Moses may be so well known to us that we overlook the implications for us. If God is "merciful" and "forgiving" we should take confidence that our sins are forgiven. In fact, drawing upon an understanding of God's character, John by inspiration speaks of God's justice being seen in the forgiveness of our sins (1John 1:9).

Verse 7 - "Unto the third and to the fourth generation…" might be taken as a general comment about God's longsuffering. However, the phrase is rare in Scripture, occurring here and in Exo 20:5, Num 14:18, Deut 5:9. Israel were to come out of Egypt "in the fourth generation" (Genesis 15:16), so we might say that the fourth generation was the generation that died in the wilderness., and that the third generation were punished in Egypt because they were not willing to cast away their idols (Ezekiel 20:7-8). So we see that the phrase could be a specific reference to those to whom deliverance from Egypt had been a possibility, the generation that were punished in Egypt and the generation that died in the wilderness.

Exodus 35

Resting from God's work

Moses has just come down from Mount Sinai with the law, having mediated on the people's behalf. As a result God's presence would now go with them, and they would need to build the ark and tabernacle for that to be a possibility.

> *And he said, My presence shall go with thee, and I will give thee rest. (Exo 33:14)*

Moses then repeats the law not to work on the Sabbath, just before commanding them to start building the tabernacle:

> *And Moses gathered all the congregation of the children of Israel together, and said unto them, These are the words which the LORD hath commanded, that ye should do them. Six days shall work be done, but on the seventh day there shall be to you an holy day, a sabbath of rest to the LORD: whosoever doeth work therein shall be put to death. (Exo 35:1-2)*

The fact that Moses singled out this one law indicates that they were going to be working on the tabernacle full time. This work would have the benefit of uniting the people in a common goal, but however spiritual this act of building was, God emphasised that they still needed to get their priorities right. The tabernacle would not overshadow the law that was established right the way back in creation:

> *And God blessed the seventh day, and sanctified it: because that in it he had rested from all his work which God created and made. (Gen 2:3)*

Who is the missing master craftsman?

Notice that the main craftsman for the tabernacle was Bezaleel from the tribe of Judah:

> *And Moses said unto the children of Israel, See, the LORD hath called by name Bezaleel the son of Uri, the son of Hur, of the tribe of Judah; and he hath filled him with the spirit of God, in wisdom, in understanding, and in knowledge, and in all manner of workmanship; and to devise curious works, to work in gold, and in silver, and in brass, and in the cutting of stones, to set them, and in carving of wood, to make any manner of cunning work. (Exo 35:30-33)*

and his helper was Oholiab from Dan:

> *And he hath put in his heart that he may teach, both he, and Aholiab, the son of Ahisamach, of the tribe of Dan. (Exo 35:34)*

Amazingly, when the temple was built, we find the chief craftsman was also of Dan. Notice how similar he is to Bezalel:

And now I have sent a cunning man, endued with understanding, of Huram my father's, the son of a woman of the daughters of Dan, and his father was a man of Tyre, skilful to work in gold, and in silver, in brass, in iron, in stone, and in timber, in purple, in blue, and in fine linen, and in crimson; also to grave any manner of graving, and to find out every device which shall be put to him ... (2Ch 2:13-14)

So there is a definite Biblical link between the men who built the tabernacle and the ones who built the temple. For the pattern to be complete, we should be able to find a man of the tribe of Judah in scripture who built the temple with Huram. Can you find who this man from the tribe of Judah is?

Food for thought

Verse 5 - In reading that the offerer should give with a "willing heart" we see the basis for the teaching of 2 Corinthians 9:7

Verses 10, 21-22, 25 - This chapter speaks of those who are "wise hearted" and "willing hearted". It is not sufficient to be willing to work for God. One has, also, to make sure that the work that one does is acceptable to Him. This is why it is essential that the willing one is also wise.

Exodus 36

Who gave us our ability to give?

And they received of Moses all the offering, which the children of Israel had brought for the work of the service of the sanctuary, to make it withal. And they brought yet unto him free offerings every morning. And all the wise men, that wrought all the work of the sanctuary, came every man from his work which they made; and they spake unto Moses, saying, The people bring much more than enough for the service of the work, which the LORD commanded to make. (Exo 36:3-5)

The free-will offering of time, effort and possessions in this chapter seems remarkable. But should it seem remarkable to us? Think of the context of what had just happened.

- The people had been slaves in a foreign land, possibly all their lives.
- They had been working from dusk till dawn, latterly in poor conditions.
- They had been made entirely free of that burden.
- They had been fed and watered in the wilderness, and promised their own country.

When the children of Israel were slaves they had very little. Now God had given them great riches by spoiling the Egyptians:

> *And the children of Israel did according to the word of Moses; and they borrowed of the Egyptians jewels of silver, and jewels of gold, and raiment: and the LORD gave the people favour in the sight of the Egyptians, so that they lent unto them such things as they required. And they spoiled the Egyptians. (Exo 12:35-36)*

So perhaps we can see things from their perspective: suddenly, and freely, they had been given everything - freedom, a nation, laws, food, money, riches, safety. They were giving some of it back to God out of joy and gratitude.

Perhaps this is a good pattern for us to think about in regard to our own lives too. Everything we have is from God, and He has promised us so much more. It is not remarkable that people, blessed as we are, should wish to give freely, out of joy and gratitude.

> *Every man according as he purposeth in his heart, so let him give; not grudgingly, or of necessity: for God loveth a cheerful giver. And God is able to make all grace abound toward you; that ye, always having all sufficiency in all things, may abound to every good work ... being enriched in every thing to all bountifulness, which causeth through us thanksgiving to God. (2Co 9:7-8, 11)*

Above all, God wishes us to be thankful. Saying "thank you" daily in prayer (and in song if we have the ability) is what we owe God for His goodness toward us:

> *Therefore by [Jesus] let us continually offer the sacrifice of praise to God, that is, the fruit of our lips, giving thanks to His name.*

But do not forget to do good and to share, for with such sacrifices God is well pleased. (Heb 13:15-16 NKJV)

Food for thought

Verse 2 - Do we ever feel "stirred up" to work with our fellow believers? That is, do we take the initiative when we see an unmet need?

Verse 35 - The veil was to separate the holy place from the most holy place in the tabernacle. It was made very carefully with skill, even though it was not seen by anyone except the priest who entered into the tabernacle. The veil represented Jesus' flesh (Heb 10:19-22). Access to the presence of God in the tabernacle was though the veil. Access to God is now through the sacrifice of Jesus.

Exodus 37

Gold that perishes

Notice the engineering detail that went into the design of the tabernacle furniture.

> *And he cast for it four rings of gold, and put the rings on the four corners that were at its four legs. The rings were close to the frame, as holders for the poles to bear the table. (Exo 37:13-14 NKJV)*

In this verse we read that the rings were "close to the frame". This means that the carrying poles lifted against the frame, not the rings. So the rings (made of relatively soft gold) weren't broken. Their function, rather than to support the table, was to hold the poles to the table when it was at rest - a much less strenuous function. Similarly for the incense altar, the rings were "under its molding", so as not to snap with the forces exerted.

> *And he overlaid it with pure gold: its top, its sides all around, and its horns. He also made for it a molding of gold all around it. He made two rings of gold for it under its molding, by its two corners*

on both sides, as holders for the poles with which to bear it. (Exo 37:26-27 NKJV)

Furthermore, the materials used are perfect for the intended purpose. The mercy seat, being pure gold, was essentially everlasting, since gold does not corrode.

Yet despite the longevity of the ark and the mercy seat, the commentary about gold in the New Testament is that it too perishes. These things were still only a foreshadowing of the true everlasting life, which is given to those who have faith in the Son of God:

> *... that the trial of your faith, being much more precious than of gold that perisheth, though it be tried with fire, might be found unto praise and honour and glory at the appearing of Jesus Christ. (1Pe 1:7)*

Food for thought

Verse 1 - Bezalel, as the one who is recorded as making the various items of the tabernacle, represents Jesus, who is building the congregation of believers according to God's instruction. The main difference being that we and our behaviour often get in the way of what Jesus is building! Eph 5:25-27

Verse 5 - Here the phrase "to bear the ark" (see also in verses 14 and 15) emphasises that the furniture of the tabernacle was to be carried. This means that the tabernacle did not have a settled resting place. In fact God reminded David of this (2Sam 7:7), which forces us to appreciate the transient and sojourning nature of Israel – a pattern of our lives in Christ. We must take care not to think of ourselves as being settled in this world.

Exodus 38

How events are foretold and echoed in scripture

> *All the gold that was occupied for the work in all the work of the holy place, even the gold of the offering, was twenty and nine talents, and seven hundred and thirty shekels... (Exo 38:24)*

All the gold that was used in the work of the holy place came from free-will offerings:

> *And they came, both men and women, as many as were willing hearted, and brought bracelets, and earrings, and rings, and tablets, all jewels of gold: and every man that offered offered an offering of gold unto the LORD. (Exo 35:22)*

And this in turn had come from the Egyptians:

> *And the children of Israel did according to the word of Moses; and they borrowed of the Egyptians jewels of silver, and jewels of gold, and raiment: and the LORD gave the people favour in the sight of the Egyptians, so that they lent unto them such things as they required. And they spoiled the Egyptians. (Exo 12:35-36)*

This had been foretold by God when He spoke to Moses at the burning bush:

> *And I will give this people favour in the sight of the Egyptians: and it shall come to pass, that, when ye go, ye shall not go empty: but every woman shall borrow of her neighbour, and of her that sojourneth in her house, jewels of silver, and jewels of gold, and raiment: and ye shall put them upon your sons, and upon your daughters; and ye shall spoil the Egyptians. (Exo 3:21-22)*

... and promised to Abraham hundreds of years before:

> *And he said unto Abram, Know of a surety that thy seed shall be a stranger in a land that is not theirs, and shall serve them; and they shall afflict them four hundred years; and also that nation, whom they shall serve, will I judge: and afterward shall they come out with great substance. (Gen 15:13-14)*

So we can see that nothing is accidental in scripture, or in the purpose of God. He works things out well in advance, and uses His angels to bring about what He has purposed beforehand. The scripture is precise and consistent in the detail of what it puts forward.

And that's not all. This point now goes forward even further in time to be echoed in the Psalms:

> *They shewed his signs among them, and wonders in the land of Ham ... He brought them forth also with silver and gold: and there was not one feeble person among their tribes. Egypt was glad when they departed: for the fear of them fell upon them. (Psa 105:27, 37-38)*

And by that connection in the Psalm, showing us that Egypt descended from Ham, Noah's son and father of Canaan, we see that this goes back even further. Was Noah speaking of this when he said that Canaan (by implication, Ham) would serve Shem?

> *And Ham, the father of Canaan, saw the nakedness of his father, and told his two brethren without ... And Noah awoke from his wine, and knew what his younger son had done unto him. And he said, Cursed be Canaan; a servant of servants shall he be unto his brethren. And he said, Blessed be the LORD God of Shem; and Canaan shall be his servant. (Gen 9:22, 24-26)*

All of this is a pattern showing how God thinks and how He brings about events according to His plan and purpose. The gold and jewels of the tabernacle are but a pattern to show us how the faithful are gathered by God to make up a spiritual household, fit for Him to dwell in:

> *And they shall be mine, saith the LORD of hosts, in that day when I make up my jewels; and I will spare them, as a man spareth his own son that serveth him. (Mal 3:17)*

Food for thought

Verse 8 - The women who "assembled at the door of the tabernacle" met to do work which was not specified. They were there to cater for the practical needs of the priests. As such, they are typical of the women who ministered to Jesus (Luke 8:3), and showed that there is a need to go beyond what is commanded, and for us to look for jobs which need doing.

Verse 22 - Isn't it appropriate that a man of the tribe of Judah supervised the making of the tabernacle? Jesus, of the tribe of Judah, built the house of God, the body of believers, through his death and resurrection (Heb 3:3).

Exodus 39

The real-life image of God

> *Thus was all the work of the tabernacle of the tent of the congregation finished: and the children of Israel did according to all that the LORD commanded Moses, so did they. (Exo 39:32)*

We know from reading in the New Testament book of Hebrews that the things Moses made were "a figure for the time then present". The people of Israel weren't yet able to appreciate the necessity for holiness and purity of heart in the worship of God (as witnessed by their turning to the golden calf), so the tabernacle and furnishings were devised as a means of teaching them these things:

> *Which was a figure for the time then present, in which were offered both gifts and sacrifices, that could not make him that did the service perfect, as pertaining to the conscience; which stood only in meats and drinks, and divers washings, and carnal ordinances, imposed on them until the time of reformation. (Heb 9:9-10)*

The shortfall of the tabernacle and the service was that it could not make the server "perfect, as pertaining to the conscience". Yet to have the perfect conscience, or in other words, a conscience free from guilt, is the missing piece of the puzzle mankind has been looking for since Adam and Eve hid in the garden:

> *And the eyes of them both were opened, and they knew that they were naked; and they sewed fig leaves together, and made themselves aprons ... And he said, I heard thy voice in the garden, and I was afraid, because I was naked; and I hid myself. (Gen 3:7, 10)*

To realise one is naked, or in other words unable to come into the presence of God because of sin, is the first step, and one that the children of Israel hadn't even grasped. Hence the strong words of God, the thunder and lightning, at mount Sinai:

> *And thou shalt set bounds unto the people round about, saying, Take heed to yourselves, that ye go not up into the mount, or touch the border of it: whosoever toucheth the mount shall be surely put to death ... And it came to pass on the third day in the morning, that there were thunders and lightnings, and a thick cloud upon the mount, and the voice of the trumpet exceeding loud; so that all the people that was in the camp trembled. (Exo 19:12, 16)*

Yet the people still didn't fear enough, so God needed to warn Moses to swiftly get down the mountain and restrain them:

> *And mount Sinai was altogether on a smoke, because the LORD descended upon it in fire: and the smoke thereof ascended as the smoke of a furnace, and the whole mount quaked greatly. ... And the LORD said unto Moses, Go down, charge the people, lest they*

> *break through unto the LORD to gaze, and many of them perish. (Exo 19:18, 21)*

Even though we don't have the tabernacle, we still have to learn the same things. We can't just dream up our own image of God and worship that, as the children of Israel did at the start. We have to learn of God by reading the Bible and by humble prayer to Him, so that we learn who He is and what attitude pleases Him. For us it is much easier than for the children of Israel, because we can learn about Jesus, who embodied perfectly the attitude and character that is acceptable to God:

> *If ye had known me, ye should have known my Father also: and from henceforth ye know him, and have seen him. Philip saith unto him, Lord, shew us the Father, and it sufficeth us. Jesus saith unto him, Have I been so long time with you, and yet hast thou not known me, Philip? He that hath seen me hath seen the Father; and how sayest thou then, Shew us the Father? (Jhn 14:7-9)*

When we confess our sins, Jesus is able to intercede for us, thereby making us perfect in regard to our conscience, and in this way enter the presence of God:

> *... and having an high priest over the house of God; let us draw near with a true heart in full assurance of faith, having our hearts sprinkled from an evil conscience, and our bodies washed with pure water. (Heb 10:21-22)*

Food for thought

Verse 30 - "Holiness to the LORD" described the position of the high priest. All his life was dedicated to the service of God. This was also the responsibility of the Nazarite, and so the same phrase is used of the days of his separation (Num 6:8).

Verse 39 - In the bringing of the completed tabernacle to Moses there is a pattern of the body of believers being presented to Christ (Ephesians 5:27).

Exodus 40

A place no-one could enter

We come to the last chapter of Exodus, and the setting up of the tabernacle. Note that the tabernacle had been devised as a way for God to go with the children of Israel on their journeys, despite their human nature and sin. The people themselves recognised this, when they said that they didn't want to hear the words of the LORD directly:

> And they said unto Moses, Speak thou with us, and we will hear: but let not God speak with us, lest we die. (Exo 20:19)

This tabernacle was designed with this in mind, providing stages of separation between God (dwelling between the cherubim, over the ark) and the people camped outside. First of all, it is made quite clear that the ark was covered by the veil:

> And thou shalt put therein the ark of the testimony, and cover the ark with the vail ... And he brought the ark into the tabernacle, and set up the vail of the covering, and covered the ark of the testimony; as the LORD commanded Moses. (Exo 40:3, 21)

Then there was the door:

> And thou shalt set the altar of gold for the incense before the ark of the testimony, and put the hanging of the door to the tabernacle. (Exo 40:5)

Then there was the court and the court gate:

> And thou shalt set up the court round about, and hang up the hanging at the court gate. (Exo 40:8)

Then there was the tent and the tent covering over that:

> And he spread abroad the tent over the tabernacle, and put the covering of the tent above upon it; as the LORD commanded Moses. (Exo 40:19)

All these coverings, gates, doors, tent and the veil, showed that God was inaccessible to the children of Israel, as they had requested. In order to commune with God, they had to go through the priesthood, who themselves had a set time and a set way to approach before the Holy Place.

When the tabernacle was fully set up, it was anointed with oil, to show that it was now holy:

> And thou shalt take the anointing oil, and anoint the tabernacle, and all that is therein, and shalt hallow it, and all the vessels thereof: and it shall be holy. (Exo 40:9)

The priests were also anointed:

> *And thou shalt put upon Aaron the holy garments, and anoint him, and sanctify him; that he may minister unto me in the priest's office. And thou shalt bring his sons, and clothe them with coats: and thou shalt anoint them, as thou didst anoint their father, that they may minister unto me in the priest's office: for their anointing shall surely be an everlasting priesthood throughout their generations. (Exo 40:13-15)*

What does all this mean? It means that the way to the LORD God was closed to normal men and women. It means that, once anointed, only the priesthood was allowed to minister before the LORD. And this is shown most strikingly in what happened next. Because when the Glory of the LORD entered the tabernacle, even Moses, who had set it up, could not enter it:

> *And Moses was not able to enter into the tent of the congregation, because the cloud abode thereon, and the glory of the LORD filled the tabernacle. (Exo 40:35)*

We, and the children of Israel at the time, are being helped to understand that, because of sin, we are unable to be in the presence of God. It is only by the priesthood of Jesus, who has entered the most holy place to be in the presence of God, that we are now privileged to have access to the LORD God through Jesus.

We need to learn that access to God is not a matter of rushing up the mountain as some of the Israelites would have tried to do. It is not a matter of making a god in the likeness we dreamed up ourselves, as they did with the golden calf. Access to God is granted to us if we are holy and blameless, and, given our human nature and sin, this can only be achieved by the forgiveness granted through our Lord Jesus Christ:

For Christ is not entered into the holy places made with hands, which are the figures of the true; but into heaven itself, now to appear in the presence of God for us: (Heb 9:24)

Food for thought

Verse 2 - So the tabernacle was set up one year after Israel left Egypt. As they arrived at Sinai three months after leaving Egypt (Exo 19:1) we know that it took them less than nine months to make the tabernacle.

Verses 3-9 - Notice the repetition of "thou". Despite the fact that others had made the tabernacle and all its furniture it was the responsibility of Moses to arrange it according to God's command. We must all work to build up the house of God – the family of believers. However, Jesus is the one who is supervising it all. He is the one who will finish the house of God and present it to himself (Eph 5:25-27).

Epilogue

The tabernacle has been built, and God's presence now is with the people. But His promise to be their God is on one condition — that they obey His law. He has taken an oath from them, and they have agreed:

> And all the people answered together, and said, **All that the LORD hath spoken we will do.** And Moses returned the words of the people unto the LORD. (Exo 19:8)

From now on in scripture we will see how hard it was to keep this promise, and we will see Israel fail again and again. We will see that it is impossible for mankind to be righteous before God, and that a realistic alternative is necessary.

In the Lord Jesus Christ we find the answer to this predicament. He is the High Priest who can obtain forgiveness for us and allow us to be presented as righteous — something the Law of Moses could never do. The mechanism for this is not total obedience to the Law, but faith in Jesus. Thus the book of Exodus and the further three books of the Law of Moses show us clearly our own failings, and our need for salvation by faith in Jesus our Saviour:

> But before faith came, we were kept under the law, shut up unto the faith which should afterwards be revealed. Wherefore the law was our schoolmaster to bring us unto Christ, that we might be

justified by faith. But after that faith is come, we are no longer under a schoolmaster. For ye are all the children of God by faith in Christ Jesus. (Gal 3:23-26)

Other books in the series

If you have enjoyed *Food for thought in Exodus* why not check out all our other books in the series? You could even collect them all!

The *Food for thought in the Old Testament* series aims to build up into a library of books covering each chapter of the Old Testament of the Bible.

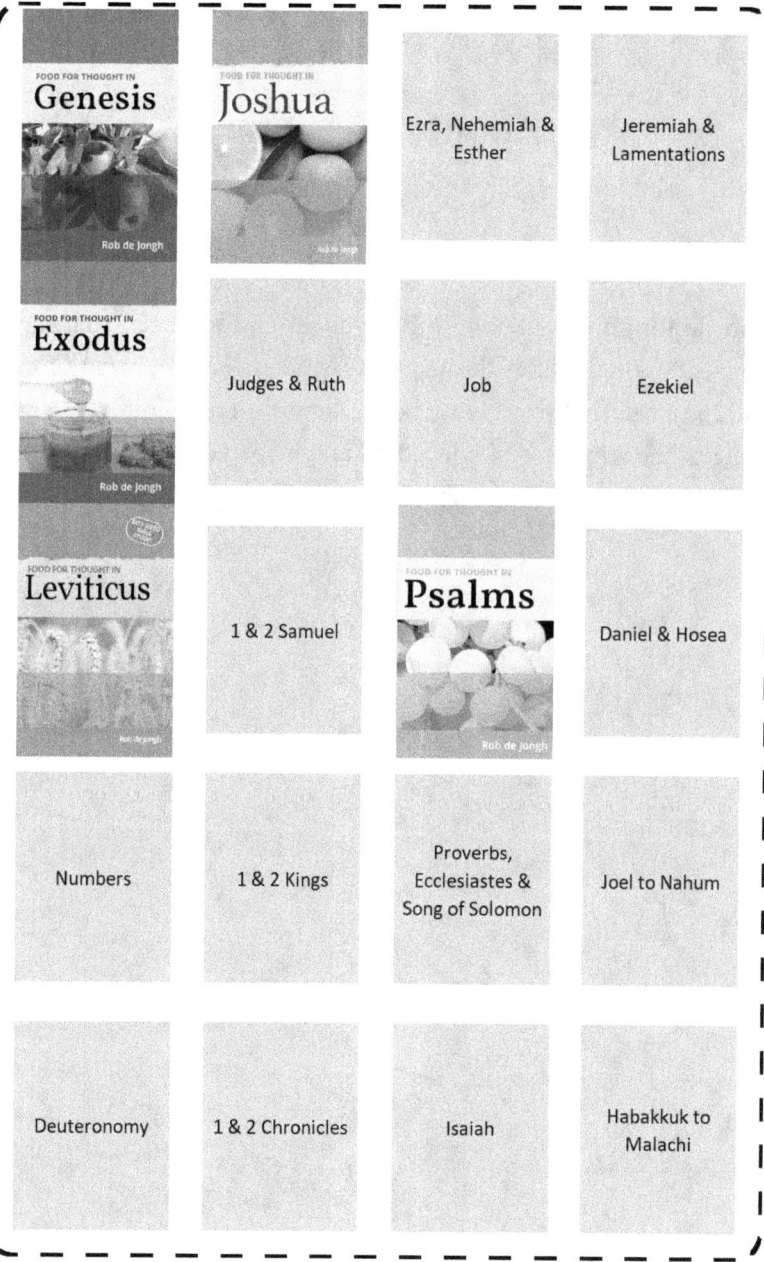

About the Author

Rob de Jongh is a lifelong Bible student and has been sharing his perspective on the Bible through talks, studies and group work for the last 25 years. He formerly worked as a non-fiction editor alongside some of the world's best educators, and helped to devise bestselling books for two successive publishers.

www.ingramcontent.com/pod-product-compliance
Lightning Source LLC
Chambersburg PA
CBHW072056110526
44590CB00018B/3193